This is a compelling story about the (that continues to claim so many youn need to know how easy it is for teer pharmaceutical opioids and how the ᵤᵣ a pandemic of epic proportions. We need public outrage to end this problem. Most importantly, we need to do our best to make sure that no other parent ever gets the call we got—that our beautiful eighteen-year-old daughter, Victoria, had died from a drug overdose. If only we had known what we know today, this tragedy might have been prevented.

David Siegel, president and CEO of Westgate Resorts, founder of Victoria's Voice Foundation, and father of Victoria "Rikki" Siegel

Rick Van Warner is a wonderful storyteller. His book reads like fiction and captures the angst in families where addiction and its collateral damage impact loved ones. In this compelling and honestly disarming family memoir revolving around his son's addiction to synthetic opioids, Rick exposes the excesses and deceptions created by Big Pharma and shows a different path to treatment and recovery than conventional wisdom allows. His contribution to the field is significant, controversial, and a real page-turner.

Mark S. Freeman, PhD, psychotherapist and counselor

This is a brutally honest account of a father's plea to a desperate son in his descent into a hell of drug addiction. This searing narrative of abiding love amid tales of pain, anger, and despair is an inspiration for all who have known the heartbreak of children stumbling down destructive paths.

Walter J. LaCentra, professor emeritus of philosophy and author of *The Authentic Self*

When OxyContin and its relatives were first introduced to my oncology practice in the late 1990s, everyone was excited by the claims of reduced-addiction risk, long duration of action, and morphine-like potency. It was only years later that we realized the information provided by the pharmaceutical reps was misleading and that this drug was highly addictive. *On Pills and Needles* shows how one family (and by extension, society) was affected by Big Pharma greed and ignorance. This is an excellent read, and I highly recommend it to everyone, not just those affected by the ongoing opioid epidemic.

David K. Smith, MD, medical oncologist

I've known Rick and his family for more than twenty-five years. I saw firsthand the ongoing, gut-wrenching trials and tribulations they went through to save their son. *On Pills and Needles* tells the disturbing story of how prescription opioids were marketed as nonaddictive and allowed to flood the nation for more than a decade before lawmakers began recognizing a major problem. Through sharing his family's fight to save their son, Rick paints a sad portrait of a national epidemic that continues to kill thousands each year. This book is a story about a national darkness, personal courage, and a family's perseverance and refusal to give up on their son in the face of heartbreaking challenges.

Richard Walsh, CEO, The Knob Hill Companies

How Rick and his family survived their son's heartbreaking and gut-wrenching addiction to opioids is a story that is nothing short of horrific, yet ultimately inspirational. It is one man's blind determination as a father to save his son. This is the story today's politicians should be reading.

David Katz, CEO, Elvis Duran Group

Rick Van Warner is a loving father and a gifted writer. I have known him throughout his journey with his son's addiction, and he has done everything possible to help. I am excited that he has now written a book to share his moving story and considerable learnings. It has the potential to save many people from going through the agony Rick's family has endured.

Kim Lopdrup, CEO, Red Lobster Seafood Co.

Anyone wanting perspective on the toll opioid addiction takes on the entire family and the epic struggle to overcome the devastation it causes will find Rick's book compelling. Rick writes in an open, honest, and often vulnerable way in detailing the emotional turmoil for himself, his family, and his addicted son. He discusses, in his frank way, the numerous treatment centers and therapeutic approaches that seemed to offer hope but too often turned into sources of despair. Helplessness and powerlessness were a given. Yet somehow Rick's, his family's, and his son's heroic struggles bore fruit. As a psychologist, I use the term *heroic* because that's what they were and still are.

David Carter, psychologist

Every branch in my family tree has addiction hanging like kudzu from it. And this plague is not only present today but goes back as far as I can decipher from the letters and records of my ancestors' lives. So I opened Rick's book with some concern that I would once again be battered by memories past and situations current. Instead, I found a fellow traveler, a friend who, instead of offering solutions, lent me another perspective. I recommend this book to anyone who has ever had a connection to addiction. Rick's net point, that "love and presence conquer all," may be as old as the sacred writings but is brought up-to-date in suburban Orlando.

Tim McCarthy, founder of The Business of Good Foundation and
author of Empty Abundance

Has there ever been a more timely publication of what will surely be a lifesaving book? Rick Van Warner not only takes us through the dangerous back streets of opioid addiction in America but also through the inner chambers of a loving parent's heart. I found myself holding my breath until the very last page, and when I finished I felt like I'd forever be a better person, parent, and friend. I learned a lot about opioid addiction but much more about love.

Bill Shore, CEO and founder of Share Our Strength

This book has opened my eyes to a world that I knew existed but had no understanding of. As a parent, I am frightened by the influences my child faces and the strength he needs to avoid being lured into the world of drugs and dependency. As a professional, I am now wondering who is silently suffering from dependency in my organization. We definitely plan on using Rick as our guide to navigate through these issues, help those in our care and employ who are struggling, and keep them from succumbing to the influence of opiate painkillers and drugs.

Jim Crystal, founder of The Revelry Group

This riveting tale tells about the struggle and emotional toll addiction takes on not just its victims but also their families and friends. In one of the most vivid, in-depth ways ever told, Rick Van Warner provides an absolute must-read for anyone who has dealt or is currently dealing with the realm of addiction.

Brandon Steiner, CEO and founder of Steiner Sports Marketing

This story is so powerful that, as the father of three girls, I found it challenging to read. This issue is in front of us every day, and to know that this actually happened to one of my close friends and associates is staggering. Working in the nonprofit community, I feel it's so important for people like Rick to share their stories so that families can better support each other and help identify serious issues before they become deadly. Kudos to Rick for sharing, for reaching deep within himself to bring this story to life to help others.

Scott Pansky, cofounder of Allison+Partners

On Pills and Needles is a must-read for every loving parent, with important insight into how kids become addicts and how families might fight and love their way to survival. This is a story as harrowing as it is ultimately hopeful. As our nation grapples with opiate addiction, this brave father shares his family's story with brutal honesty—one family's road map out of hell. It is fast-paced, beautifully written, and incredibly moving.

The story Rick tells is immensely personal, but it also touches every family in America. The scourge of prescription drug abuse and the tragic consequences it too often sadly leads to for both teenagers and adults need to be addressed with courage and commitment. As hard as it may be to start, we all need to read this powerful message and join the fight to save our families and friends. Thanks for your strength, Rick.

Christopher Muller, PhD, friend and business colleague

In writing *On Pills and Needles*, Rick Van Warner has provided us with a compelling and unique perspective of the opioid epidemic in the United States. Over a decade of his and his family's life has been focused on his dear son's addiction, dealing with self-doubt, strains on marriage, balancing the needs of other children, financial considerations, and much more. Moreover, as a medical professional, I cannot help but be impressed with the depth of research and truth this volume has provided for myself, my colleagues, and the lay public. It is no less a journey of unconditional fatherly love and discipline, a roller-coaster ride accompanied by unfathomable pain and resentment shifting to forgiveness, acceptance, and encouragement as key scaffolds in the bridge to a sustained recovery.

Kerry M. Schwartz, MD, FACC, FACP, clinical and interventional cardiologist, Orlando, Florida

On Pills and Needles is a brilliantly written account of one family's life-and-death battle with opioid addiction. Rick Van Warner maintains the fast-paced intensity of a Grisham novel as he unravels this personal journey through the swirling path of his son's addiction. We're not just along for the ride; we're riding shotgun as we discover the pandemic reach of this addiction—the loss of more than ninety American lives every day and the impact on countless others. We're both informed and inspired as we see the heartbreak that opioid addiction has brought on his entire family. Rick's battle becomes a bigger war, as he discovers the stranglehold that greedy Big Pharma and their lobbyists maintain, thus blocking any meaningful legislation that could end this atrocity. I highly recommend that you and everyone you know read this book. Share it with your family, friends, and neighbors. You might change a life, or at least educate a community, and help solve one of the biggest problems out there.

Richard G. Rosen, chief architect of convergence marketing, speaker, and author of *Convergence Marketing: Combining Brand and Direct for Unprecedented Profits*

ON PILLS
AND NEEDLES

ON PILLS
AND NEEDLES

The Relentless Fight to Save My Son
from Opioid Addiction

RICK VAN WARNER

BakerBooks

a division of Baker Publishing Group
Grand Rapids, Michigan

© 2018 by Rick Van Warner

Published by Baker Books
a division of Baker Publishing Group
PO Box 6287, Grand Rapids, MI 49516-6287
www.bakerbooks.com

Printed in the United States of America

Library of Congress Cataloging-in-Publication Data
Names: Van Warner, Rick, 1961– author.
Title: On pills and needles : the relentless fight to save my son from opioid addiction
     / Rick Van Warner.
Description: Grand Rapids, MI : Baker Books, [2018] | Includes bibliographical
     references.
Identifiers: LCCN 2017035030 | ISBN 9780801075353 (paper)
Subjects: LCSH: Van Warner, Tommy—Mental health. | Opioid abuse—Patients—
     United States—Biography. | Opioid abuse—Treatment—Family relationships.
Classification: LCC RC568.O45 V36 2018 | DDC 362.29/3092 [B] —dc23
LC record available at https://lccn.loc.gov/2017035030

Some names and details have been changed to protect the privacy of the individuals involved.

18 19 20 21 22 23 24   7 6 5 4 3 2

To my son Tommy,
whose courage, resilience, wit, and huge heart
continue to inspire me.

CONTENTS

ACKNOWLEDGMENTS

With tremendous gratitude, love, and thanks to my beautiful wife, Mary, whose pioneer spirit, love for her family, and unwavering support and belief in me made this book possible. The love of my life has been our family's rock—through all the good times and the bad—and has been an incredible mother, partner, and friend. Your caring nature and determination have always sustained me.

A special thanks to our three incredible young men and awesome daughter, who each day bring light into our lives and the lives of others. I love each of you more than you will ever know.

Heartfelt thanks to my brother, Ron, who selflessly took our son under his wing on several occasions and provided endless hours of support and encouragement along the way. Thanks also to my mother, Isabel, who offered love and encouragement to her grandson during the periods he lived under her and his uncle's roof.

Special thanks to my mother-in-law, Donatella, who took our son in several times during periods when he had nowhere else to go and who was a constant source of love and support for her grandson, even though his parents often disagreed with her decisions.

Thanks to my friends Bobby C. and Mike and all of my other brothers in life, men who were always there to offer encouragement and perspective. The friendships and bonds we continue to share are truly remarkable and have positively transformed my life. Thanks also to the many other friends who stepped up over the years to lend their love and support to Mary and me during challenging times.

Thank you to my therapist and friend, Dr. David C., whose wise counsel and insights have enhanced my life and whose sense of humor has shown me that not all shrinks are full of it!

Sincere thanks to my dear friends Ed and Edye, Brian and Rachel, Jan, and Bobby C., who generously afforded me the opportunity to find solace and draw inspiration from gorgeous mountain, ocean, and lakeside views while writing from their various abodes.

Thanks to my agent, Leila, for taking a chance and opening my eyes to a path I hadn't initially recognized, and to my friends Dave A., Ernie, and Anya, who helped guide me toward her doorstep. And thank you to my dear, longtime friends Dave K., Roxanne, Mary Ellen, and Suzanne and to my new friend Susan K., whose encouragement and insights helped me to overcome nagging insecurities and to complete this book.

Finally, thanks to God for opening my eyes and ignoring my stubbornness while patiently reminding me of the purpose he has always had for my life.

INTRODUCTION

We found him curled up in a fetal position on the concrete floor of an abandoned, multistory military barracks, alone except for the broken glass, empty medicine bottles, and lurid graffiti covering the walls. A disillusioned, broken teenager, he was barely breathing, the hood of his black sweatshirt hiding the pain and confusion lying deep behind inflated black pupils that nearly blotted out his hazel eyes. Through the drug-induced haze of his fourth escape from reality in as many days, he lay motionless, staring straight ahead, not even recognizing the sound of his older brother's voice.

How could this possibly have happened, I wondered in relief, sadness, and terror. How had the most gentle and caring of our three sons, the laid-back boy with the easy smile and open heart, been reduced to an emotionless runaway, the self-inflicted lighter burns on his body a testament to an indifference to pain, living, or dying? How could this sixteen-year-old, who less than a week earlier had left home on a typical Friday morning for school, now be flirting with death by overdose?

Much has been written and many parental hands wrung over the perils of growing up in a digital world in which incessant Snapchats and selfies seem to have replaced interpersonal connections or conversations, even when both parties are in the same room. What has been lost when teenagers no longer have the patience or courage to drop their social media personas long enough to share face-to-face conversations about their insecurities and challenges with others going through the same thing? Meanwhile, constant digital access has created a false expectation within many businesses of 24/7 availability, further reducing time for focused interpersonal interactions within families.

This current state of human impatience and dysfunction has made our world tougher than ever before, especially for teens and young adults searching for their identity and niche. But the plague of addiction claiming a growing number of our kids stretches far beyond the pervasive influence of digital media, disconnected parents, and typical teen angst.

Since the dawn of the new millennium, an unprecedented prescription pain pill and heroin epidemic has been claiming American lives—including a disproportionate number of teens and young adults—at an alarming rate. Spawned by big pharmaceutical corporation greed and deception, this growing epidemic kills over ninety Americans per day, the CDC reports, eclipsing auto accidents as the nation's leading cause of accidental death. With the possible exception of methamphetamine, no substance can create dependency and ensnare a user in its deadly grip more quickly than oxycodone—the primary ingredient in OxyContin and copycat drugs—and its older cousin heroin. Even those experimenting just a few times, perhaps idolizing such media-celebrated heroin heroes as Kurt Cobain, can quickly and unexpectedly find themselves stuck in the powerful web of addiction. Sadly, death or jail is often the only way heroin or synthetic heroin's grip can be broken for many addicts. Those who can afford rehabilitation programs or seek recovery through state-funded centers typically do so repeatedly, only to relapse again and again.

How this deadly public health crisis grew to today's epic proportions is maddening, particularly for those of us grappling with the agonizing journey of trying to keep a loved one alive. Similar to the nation's financial crisis from 2007 to 2009, lax oversight by government regulators beholden to powerful corporate lobby interests allowed the addictive pain pill problem to grow unchecked for more than a decade. For years Big Pharma lobbyists threw millions of dollars at politicians and regulators to look the other way, and it wasn't until staggering numbers of teens and twenty-somethings began overdosing and dying that officials finally took action, inadvertently worsening the problem by pushing it from pharmacies into the alleys. Street dealers were more than happy to serve this new generation of opiate dependents, providing inexpensive heroin and copycat oxycodone pills, both often cut with deadly chemicals. This shift from Mom's medicine cabinet to the street has mostly just poured gas onto a spreading wildfire that shows no signs of abating.

In Florida, ground zero for a synthetic heroin (aka Oxy) crisis that eventually spread to all fifty states, more than 650 million oxycodone-based pills flooded the market by 2010, leading to most of the state's 1,516 overdose deaths that year. While three of our four children were coming of age during their middle and high school years, pain clinics known as *pill mills* were popping up like dandelions after a hard rain throughout our region. Unscrupulous doctors, many with mail-order degrees, gladly lined their pockets by doling out scripts to anyone who had cash, credit, or Medicaid.

On streets and in schools, Oxys became inexpensive and easy to find. Disenfranchised and bored teens learned that crushing the pills into a powder that could be snorted, injected, or smoked neutralized the time-release mechanism, creating an intense and nearly immediate escape from reality. Odorless and hard to detect, the pills became a recreational favorite, especially for disillusioned kids who struggled to find their group or feel accepted. The drugs did not discriminate, and kids and adults from all types of social and economic backgrounds soon became hooked.

The pain any of us with an addict in our life must endure, whether we are a parent, child, sibling, spouse, or friend, is the harsh reality that we are powerless to alter the course of their path. Only the person suffering from drug dependency can change course, leaving the rest of us in their chaotic wake as cringing observers. Like a car crash on the highway, we don't really want to look but have no choice.

As the father of three young men and a daughter, and as a son who has spent a lifetime recovering from psychological wounds inflicted during childhood from an abusive, alcoholic father, the particularly complex dynamic between fathers and children plays an important role in the stories shared in this book. The complicated, intertwining relationship between substance abuse and mental disorders is also an important topic, based on practical perspectives gained over several long and often agonizing years of trying to save our son versus any formal psychological schooling.

This arduous journey has taken us through numerous twelve-step meetings, residential and outpatient recovery programs, and therapist offices, and we've come to understand that a person's individual psyche and will to change is the only chance they have to overcome addiction. Most people accept the medical definition of addiction as a "disease," but as the years passed, I grew to detest this label as far too simplistic for the incredibly complex stew of brain chemistry, socialization, genetic predisposition, and life experience that leads to substance abuse. One size does not fit all, and there are no easy solutions when it comes to addiction.

In our case, we discovered that our family's unconditional love and acceptance proved far more powerful than any programs, group therapy sessions, medicines, or doctors in helping our son survive. Only by putting conventional wisdom aside and accepting our son with love, no matter what, were we able to help him inch forward. Tough love and detachment proved highly overrated with our tremendously sensitive son, serving only to push him to the brink.

The razor-thin line between love and boundaries is a difficult balancing act, and by no means does this book purport to offer the solution to this terrible problem or suggest that new or unique expertise can be found within its pages. It was written with a sincere desire to help others survive the trials of parenting, coping with an addict, or simply navigating life itself. By sharing the raw, honest experiences and mistakes made while engulfed in our son's battle, along with the seemingly endless mental struggle to regain hope, we wish to offer a small measure of solace to others stumbling down the same road.

1

THE VANISHING

As darkness fell on the day after Tommy disappeared, his mother became increasingly anxious when her call to his phone went straight to voicemail.

"I've got a really bad feeling," Mary said. "Where could he be?"

It wasn't unusual for my worrisome wife to jump to conclusions that could inject panic into nearly any situation. But this time, I shared her dread.

"Calm down, you always imagine the worst," I replied, ignoring the growing ball of tension in my stomach. "I'm sure he just went to hang out with a friend. He knew he was grounded if he came home, so it shouldn't be a shock that he didn't show after all we've been through this week."

She glared back at me. "What if you're wrong?"

Tommy choosing not to ride the bus that day was not that surprising, since this was humiliating to a high school junior who had been driving himself to school since the previous semester. Losing driving privileges was one of several punishments leveled due to his abysmal behavior of late, which included failing home drug tests, cursing at his parents, not coming home by curfew, and being arrested with a friend for stealing change and electronic devices out of unlocked cars. When you've taken every possible privilege away and essentially have a child on permanent lockdown except to attend school or a job, it is very hard to determine what to do next.

By now we had visited doctors and therapists and had tried to reach Tommy in every way possible, but emotionless detachment had replaced his sensitive and silly nature. The defiant, stone-faced look he now always gave us was both disturbing and maddening. He simply no longer cared, as if to say, "There's nothing more you can do to me, so screw you!"

As we learned later, Tommy was among a growing number of kids that had discovered they could experience euphoric escape from whatever pain or insecurities they wrestled with by crushing prescription painkillers known as Oxys into powder they could then snort, smoke, or inject.

With the twentieth century winding down and doomsday techies beginning to warn about the imminent Y2K threat, Connecticut-based pharmaceutical company Purdue Pharma[1] won FDA approval for a new pain pill containing oxycodone. OxyContin, unlike earlier oxycodone-based painkillers that had been used in the United States for nearly fifty years, promised up to twelve hours of relief due to "revolutionary" time-release advancements that eliminated the highly addictive qualities associated with traditional painkillers such as Percodan or morphine.

After winning FDA approval in 1996, Purdue launched a massive sales and marketing campaign deceptively centered on the wonder drug's "nonaddictive" qualities. Purdue's principal owners, three brothers who were all psychiatrists, had earlier discovered the power and profits possible through marketing directly to doctors to influence the pharmaceuticals they prescribed. The eldest was both a psychiatrist and the lead ad man behind the rise of Valium to become the first drug to surpass $100 million in sales, an achievement that won him induction into the Medical Advertising Hall of Fame. The brothers' pioneering efforts to market to and incentivize doctors to prescribe their products essentially created the Big Pharma sales model that exists today.

Long before *big data* was a marketing term, Purdue was leveraging sophisticated market-by-market databases to target doctors who would be most likely to prescribe their pain pill, focusing their efforts on those who historically were most liberal in writing scripts for opioids.[2] Between 1996 and 2001, Purdue hosted more than forty national pain-management and speaker-training conferences at resorts in Florida, California, and Arizona, all-expenses-paid boondoggles designed to influence their highest potential prescribers and deputize attending doctors, pharmacists, and nurses to spread the word about OxyContin.[3] By 2007 more than seventy-five tons of synthetic opioids were being manufactured worldwide, with the United States accounting for 82 percent of consumption, according to the International Narcotics Control Board.

Purdue also more than doubled their on-the-ground sales force, with sales reps swarming doctors' offices across the nation to push their new wonder drug, rewarding lucrative bonuses to reps with the most success. The OxyContin pushers were well armed. A starter-coupon program offered patients free limited-time prescriptions for a seven-to-thirty-day supply, enough to create initial dependency for some. OxyContin fishing hats, plush toys, and a distasteful "Get in the Swing with OxyContin" music CD were in the giveaway mix.

The efforts by Purdue clearly worked. By the turn of the century, OxyContin sales exceeded $1 billion (topping $35 billion to date), and by 2001 Purdue was spending more than $200 million per year marketing it as the drug of choice for everything from wisdom teeth removal to lower back pain. According to the US Department of Health and Human Services, between 1999 and 2010, sales of opioid pain meds nearly quadrupled, as did the number of opioid overdose deaths. By 2012, doctors wrote more than 282 million opioid painkiller prescriptions.[4]

When Tommy entered high school in 2007, the epidemic in Florida was in full swing. By 2010 Florida pharmacies were churning out 650 million opioid pills per year, with ninety-three of the top one hundred oxycodone-dispensing doctors in the United States working in the Sunshine State.[5] More than half of the pills were not used by the patients who filled their prescriptions, research suggests. Instead, the plastic bottles were regularly left half or three-quarters full in the medicine cabinets of mothers, fathers, aunts, uncles, and grandparents, who might have taken a few after a minor surgery but disliked how the pills made them feel and quit taking them after a day or two. With the pills now fetching $5 or more each, kids soon learned how easy it was to steal a few of the forgotten pills from the bathrooms of family members or friends. In the halls of high schools and middle schools, Oxys became "as easy to get as candy at a 7-Eleven," a police officer told me during one of many incidents involving my son. Two out of three teens who abuse the drugs obtained them from family or friends,[6] and 80 percent of heroin users started out using nonmedical prescription opioids before progressing to heroin, according to the National Institute on Drug Abuse.[7] Florida, one of the least restrictive in the union when it comes to government regulation, did not have an electronic prescription tracking program in place at the time, a measure several other states had successfully deployed to curb prescription drug abuse. All this created a perfect storm. Nearly anyone could easily get a prescription from a pain clinic doctor that they could then fill as many times as desired at various pharmacies. More and more Floridians, including a disproportionate number of younger residents, soon became hooked on the white or colored pills.

A self-absorbed generation of parents was initially oblivious to the growing problem, which was far more difficult to detect than marijuana or alcohol use given the absence of odor or signs of intoxication. By 2014, some fifteen million Americans aged twelve and older were using the prescription drugs recreationally, the US Department of Health and Human Services reported.[8]

Demonstrating the widening gap between perception and reality, a Partnership for Drug-Free Kids study found that 95 percent of parents believed their child had never used a prescription drug recreationally, yet 25 percent of teens reported having done so, beginning as young as age twelve.[9] Initially it seemed that the only ones who understood the spreading problem were those on the front lines left to deal with the consequences: police officers knocking on doors in the middle of the night to let parents know their child had overdosed, EMTs and paramedics trying to keep someone alive in their ambulances, emergency room doctors fighting to treat a largely untreatable patient.[10] Despite clear warnings from the law enforcement and medical communities that society had a huge and growing problem to address, Big Pharma–backed lawmakers and regulators turned a blind eye to the situation.

It was during this period of public inertia and ignorance that Tommy graduated from pot and alcohol to Oxys, marking the start of his descent into the abyss. We too were mostly clueless about the destructive forces our son and family were facing or how bad things would eventually get.

The night before Tommy disappeared had been a particularly bad blowout, with me losing my cool and regressing to one of my late father's meanest traits, name-calling. It was not the first time this had happened. In fact, as much as I fought to break the cycle of yelling and verbal abuse that I'd endured myself, there were times I failed.

After picking Tommy up from his job at a sub shop, it was clear that he was completely stoned. His report card days earlier showed plummeting grades, and I sensed that drug use was behind his defiance and lack of motivation.

"What's going on with you?" I asked on the ride home.

"Nothing, why?" he replied.

"It's like you've thrown in the towel since quitting the crew team. Your grades have slipped, and it seems like all you want to do is go to your friend's house."

"Okay, Dad, you're right, I'm giving up," he replied, not trying to disguise his sarcasm.

"Don't be a smart-ass," I said. "I'm worried about you."

"Don't worry, as soon as I save up enough money I'm going to get my own place, and you won't have to worry anymore; I won't be around to bother you."

"That's not what I'm saying, Tommy. I'm trying to figure out what's going through your mind and want to help you."

"You want to help me?" he snarled. "You and Mom need to stop asking me so many questions!"

After dinner, I was pulling into the driveway after a brief errand when I saw my youngest son, Barry, then fourteen, put something in the garbage can that was next to the street for collection day, then run back through the garage. Suspicious, I parked and looked inside the can. On top of the tied trash bags was an unopened red can of Coca-Cola, which felt full when I picked it up. On closer inspection on my garage workbench, I realized that the metal top actually twisted off, revealing a hard plastic canister inside with a bag of marijuana concealed inside it. I immediately lost my cool. Barry had now somehow gotten caught up in Tommy's nonsense, I thought, storming in the house to confront Tommy.

"What the hell is this?" I demanded. "And why are you having Barry do your dirty work for you? Is he smoking pot too?" My fears were not unfounded, as I learned years later that Tommy had introduced both his older and younger brothers to occasional pot smoking during their high school years, but thankfully no other drugs.

"It's a Coke can," Tommy replied, defiantly looking me in the eyes as if to say, *Go ahead, what are you going to do to me?* By now all his privileges had been removed.

"Listen, this has to stop now!" I shouted. "It's bad enough that you're turning into a loser, now you want to drag your brother down with you?"

"Whatever," he said, attempting to walk away. I grabbed him by the shoulder and spun him around to face me.

"Don't you walk away from me, smart-ass!" I yelled. By now Mary, Barry, and young Jessie were observing my temper tantrum, and latest loud argument with Tommy, from up the hall. "This is our house, and you're going to live by our rules. Get it?"

"Fine," he said without a hint of remorse.

Repressed anger is like a vicious, caged animal, ready to slash and gore anyone within striking distance on the awful, embarrassing occasions it breaks free. It repulses and disgusts me, and is always immediately followed by sincere regret and apologies to those I've unintentionally hurt. Yet as hard as I try to overcome my inner anger, it still lurks in my battle-scarred subconscious. Only through counseling and faith have I found sustained periods of peace.

My son's blank stare and lack of response had been infuriating, and all the angst and worry that had been building over his erratic behavior boiled over that night. Words hurt much more than physical punches or slaps, as sadly both my sons and I know. Thankfully, I've gotten better at muting this ugly side of myself with age and have become more adept at beating back the beast during the heated moments when it seems ready to burst through the cage door. While the name-calling associated with my moronic outbursts stopped some time ago, rarely a week goes by that I don't loathe myself over the damage this might have caused to my sons. It took subsequent years of Tommy's detoxes, rehabs, and relapses, and the work I did on myself through support meetings, therapy, and reading, to eventually let myself off the hook. In retrospect, I had far less impact on his decision to disappear that fateful Friday than I then imagined.

"Relax," I told my wife, still trying to calm her as the night got darker. "He'll be home in the morning or sometime tomorrow. It's not the first time he hasn't come home, but he always comes back the next day and apologizes."

"I don't think he will this time," she said.

"He will," I assured her.

He didn't.

As Saturday evening approached, my temporary relief over not having our unmotivated, defiant son in our house began to turn into genuine concern, although I was not yet ready to share this with Mary. My mind raced with terror over finding him dead by an overdose or from violence or even suicide. As darkness fell we decided we must act.

We enlisted the help of our youngest son, Barry, and thanks to Facebook, we found that our son had spent the previous night at the house of an older girl he'd recently started seeing. It turned out that my wife had found the same girl hiding next to my son's bed at 4:00 a.m. a week earlier—having snuck in through his window after we'd gone to sleep. The girl popped up from the floor that night, extended her hand with a smile and said, "Nice to meet you, Mrs. Van Warner," and then lied about her name.

Tonight my wife insisted that we storm the girl's house, and within thirty minutes I was knocking on her front door. Her older brother, who answered suspiciously, claimed not to have seen Tommy. The two siblings, eighteen and twenty, apparently lived in this rented house by themselves, courtesy of a parent who was either disconnected or had given up hope. After scanning the place for hiding spots and finding no clues, we left.

After receiving a new tip, we drove to the home of another of Tommy's friends and spoke with the friend's mother.

"I haven't seen him since last weekend, and Max is grounded. They're all smoking way too much pot, and I'm worried they're also experimenting with other drugs."

This was not a shock since our son had already tested positive for opiates once, and we had found two white pills, which we later identified online as OxyContin, stashed under his lava lamp. His friend began telephoning mutual friends while we were speaking with his mother, and before we left he gave us a tip that made our hearts sink.

"I just spoke with a friend who says he thinks he is with our friend Connor in Baldwin Park and they are robo-tripping," said Tommy's friend, who seemed as excited to unearth this clue as an explorer discovering a new island. "He says he saw them, and they're really messed up!"

We learned that it was becoming increasingly popular for kids to chug an entire bottle of Robitussin cough syrup, activating enough of its active ingredient DXM to induce a hallucinogenic trip—that is, if the user's heart didn't stop beating first. Tommy's friend suggested searching for our son in this planned community, which had been built on an old naval base in Orlando. More specifically, he added, we should check out the abandoned naval barracks there.

Thinking overdose or worse, we sprang into crisis mode. Given that it was now after 10:00 p.m. and our exhausted young daughter was with us, we decided that she and my wife would return home and I'd continue to search. Ill-prepared for what lay ahead, I grabbed a flashlight and began the twenty-minute drive to Baldwin Park, enlisting the help of my friend Rich along the way. After picking him up and explaining the situation, we headed to the abandoned building.

It was an imposing structure, rising seven stories high and longer than a football field, and completely engulfed in darkness with not even a streetlight near it. Situated in the middle of a completely overgrown, trash-strewn lot and surrounded by a chain link fence, it looked like it belonged more in a '70s-era burnt-out South Bronx neighborhood than in the middle of this manicured new development.

"What are we going to do if we find him?" Rich asked after I picked him up.

"Bring him home," I replied, not really confident this would be possible.

"But what if he doesn't want to come?" he asked, foreshadowing events that were to unfold in New Jersey less than a year later.

"I don't know."

By this point I'd already considered what might happen should Tommy refuse to come with us if found. I knew he was fast and could easily outrun either of us. But if I had the chance to get close enough, I was confident in my ability to restrain him until reinforcements arrived. After all, I outweighed him by one hundred pounds and, although out of shape, had retained much of my upper body strength from previous athletic pursuits through workouts and outdoor physical activities. The ballooning tire around my midsection would have made chase futile, but there was no way he could escape my grasp. Worst case, I'd hold him until police or medical personnel arrived with proper restraints. Nothing was going to stop me from getting him into a hospital for treatment, with the exception of leaving him an open path for escape.

Once at the site, we stepped over a section of the chain link fence that was knocked down, one of a few entry points we would later find out was used by the numerous kids who frequented this place to use drugs or escape from their parents. As we got closer to the building, it became even more imposing, massive in size and covered in graffiti. We were

31

almost immediately swept with a sense of evil, a very dark vibe I felt every time I was in close proximity to the building and a feeling so strong it resurfaced each time I drove past the monstrosity in later months.

As we navigated broken bottles and shattered glass along a sidewalk leading up to the building—in our haste to reach the destination I was still wearing flip-flops—we were overcome by fear. It was pitch dark except for the weak beams from our small flashlights, and we could see many of the windows had been broken, most covered by plywood, with police "no trespassing" warning signs stapled to the wood. As we circled the building looking for an opening to get inside, we came across two empty Robitussin cough syrup bottles on the ground. They looked new and freshly discarded, which indicated our tip was likely accurate.

Just around the corner we found an opening where a piece of the plywood had been kicked and broken off, creating an entryway into the sinister den. When we stepped inside it was even worse. The floors were strewn with broken glass, empty cans, insulation, and other debris, and more graffiti plastered the walls. We soon discovered that the place was a labyrinth of long hallways lined with rooms, supply closets, bathrooms, and stairwells, not to mention empty elevator shafts. Tommy and his friend could be anywhere, if they were here at all. So could anyone else. After calling out Tommy's name a couple times with no response and taking stock of our weak flashlights, lack of defenses, and inappropriate footwear, we decided to retreat.

Back on the street we called the police.

The first officer who arrived was bored and disinterested in our plight.

"How long has he been missing?" he asked.

"Since yesterday."

"How old is he?" the officer asked, clearly annoyed by my first answer.

"Sixteen," I replied, adding, "He didn't get off the bus after school and we haven't seen him since yesterday morning. He may be on hard drugs that can kill him!"

"Look, he'll probably come home when he gets hungry or comes down," the officer said, tucking his notepad into his pocket. "You can choose to file a missing person report, but since you don't live in this city, you'll have to do this where you live. Kids run away all the time these days, and usually they come back before long. Sorry I can't help you; good luck."

As he turned to walk back to the driver side of his cruiser, I could feel my face flushing in anger.

"You mean you won't even help us search the building?" I asked.

"Look buddy, that place is way too dangerous to search in the daytime, and certainly too dangerous to search at night. I wouldn't suggest putting anyone at risk by going in there. For one thing, you never know who could be hiding inside. I've also heard the floors are crumbling and not structurally sound. You should not go in there, and I'm certainly not going to send anyone in there. Good luck finding your son."

With that, one of Orlando's finest climbed into his car and drove away, leaving my friend and me standing on the edge of the overgrown lot, dumbfounded. The same pattern would repeat itself over the next seventy-two hours, as we tried several more times to receive assistance from the city's police department.

When you have a kid who disappears, the first thing you learn is that unless they have been gone for a long time, most police officers do not want to hear about it. With the many challenges today's police officers face, including lack of basic respect from those they serve to protect, it is understandable they are not anxious to spend time chasing runaway kids. But this does nothing to change how disheartening this was that night. We were on our own.

We combed Baldwin Park for the next few hours, asking the few people who were out if they'd seen the two boys, with one saying he had and repeating the friend's line from earlier, "They looked really messed up." Dejected and more worried than ever, I pulled into the driveway at 3:00 a.m. to give Mary the bad news.

"What do you mean you can't find him?" she demanded. "What did the police say?"

As usual, Mary's tone was shrill and accusatory, as if I'd left stones unturned or absentmindedly forgotten to mark some of the boxes on whatever checklist resided in her mind. Only recently has she become aware of how quickly her tone can spark defensive or combative responses from any of us on the receiving end. Too exhausted to be irritated, I replied, "They were not helpful at all. We need to get some sleep. Then I'll go back in the morning when it is light out."

She began sobbing, reverting to her habit of envisioning the very worst. While I fully recognized that his drug abuse might kill him, I wasn't ready to go there yet. When any such dire thought would manage to slip past the curtain of my fierce focus on finding Tommy, I'd immediately stomp it back down. Like confrontation, which I usually try to avoid— likely a result of the loud verbal warfare that dominated the house I grew up in—I subconsciously knew that allowing such thoughts any space could disrupt my ability to complete the task at hand.

"We may never see him again!" she moaned. "What did we do wrong?"

Fighting back my own tears, I did my best to comfort her before she fell asleep.

After a couple hours of restless sleep, I returned to the scene early the next morning, determined to fully search the vacant building. This time I was prepared, wearing steel-toe boots and carrying a high-powered flashlight in one hand, an aluminum baseball bat in the other, and a particularly nasty hunting knife in my pocket. In the early morning light I reentered the building, which remained mostly dark inside. Scared and alone but determined, I began searching the first floor room by room, swinging open doors to pitch-dark boiler rooms and quickly scanning the area with my flashlight beam, half-expecting someone to jump out at any second. I kept pivoting my head, certain that someone was sneaking up behind me. As I entered the black stairwell leading to the second floor, I had progressed from scared to terrified.

The higher floors of the building were each split into two wings, separated by stairwells with an elevator at either end. With no windows, the stairwells, areas outside the elevators, small broom closets, and boiler rooms on both ends of every floor were pitch black. I systematically searched each of them but found no sign of my son. Stepping to one of the outer wings was a relief by comparison, with at least some light coming through the mostly broken windows. Presumably once the sleeping quarters, each wing was about the length of two bowling alleys; massive bathrooms were located at the ends. The huge, communal, windowless bathrooms were also cloaked in darkness, making the process of pulling back every shower curtain and opening every bathroom stall door tedious and scary. In one of the bathrooms a broken mirror had a disturbing message borrowed from the horror movie *The Shining* written in what appeared to be blood, but was more likely lipstick or red spray paint—"REDRUM" (murder spelled backward).

Floor by floor my routine continued, and at any turn I half-expected to find my lifeless son on the floor. There were many signs of the drug use, drinking, and vandalism that took place here, but no indications that my son or anyone else was present this morning.

By the time I reached the top floor, sweaty and tired from my two-hour search, my fear had abated, and I was more confidently moving through the building, especially the well-lit wings. Hope that my son was likely still alive gave me relief. The entire morning I'd moved through the building in relative silence, except for the eerie creaking of metal doors I opened to peer inside and the thump of them closing behind me. As I started up the final stairwell, this one leading to the roof, a sudden explosion of sound nearly caused me to fall down the stairs. A startled pigeon flew inches over my head and away from his interior perch. Breathing a sigh of relief, I continued to the roof and found no one.

Never had the air felt so fresh and the sun so bright as when I left that decaying building and returned to my car. But I was discouraged. Perhaps Tommy wasn't here after all and was somehow on his way to California, somewhere he talked frequently about wanting to travel to. We learned later that the Golden State was also where he told friends he planned to go.

2

DESPAIR ABOARD
THE OXY EXPRESS

As I peered at Tommy's face in his recent rowing team photo used to create the missing-person flyers I was distributing, I noticed that he no longer smiled when having his picture taken. A quick glance at family photos from the past year confirmed this; he was not angry but dispassionate, offering only a blank stare of indifference. Drug use had replaced any happiness with nothingness.

On day three of our search, I began to believe that Tommy might already be far away from Orlando, although my instincts kept drawing me back to the hellish abandoned naval barracks like a magnet. Just a few weeks ago my son had been part of a crew rowing team that successfully broke and established a new indoor world record for continuous rowing on an Erg machine. It was set up in the home of one of his teammates, and the eight boys kept rowing in shifts around the clock, smoothly changing places so as to never let the machine stop turning, for ten consecutive days. The feat earned them a spot on the television news, with a remote feed on the night they broke the record, as well as subsequent national magazine and newspaper articles.

Crew, a sport in which four- or eight-man boats are propelled by teammates rowing in precise unison, was not the first team activity Tommy had gravitated toward in his longing to be part of something, to belong. Trying to follow in his older brother's footsteps and possibly to placate his father, he had tried a couple of seasons of baseball when younger. A lefty, he had a nice swing and seemed to enjoy it when coaches were lobbing in easy-to-hit strikes. His baseball career ended at age ten when he started facing kid pitchers and the prospect of getting hit by the ball.

"Do you want to play baseball this season?" I asked him one autumn.

"Do I have to hit, or can I just play the field?" he asked.

"You have to hit too," I said.

"No thanks, I don't really like baseball that much anyway," he replied.

Boy Scouts and being outdoors were the things he liked best, and he continued to progress all the way to Life Scout, just a step away from Eagle, and frequently camped with his troop. He even had his Eagle project plan approved two weeks before deciding to run away. Since several of his troop members also played soccer, he took an interest in the sport and began playing around the time he abandoned baseball. He really loved playing, and his speed helped make up for what he lacked in fundamental soccer skills. But most of all he simply loved the acceptance of being part of the team, and whenever he had a chance to get into a game, his team-mates would loudly cheer for him to score.

At the same time Tommy was wrestling with the typical teen struggle of forging an identity and finding a group to belong to, Florida's opiate epidemic was growing like wildfire, with the insidious pill-mill industry stoking the flames. With new pain clinics proliferating like rats, deaths by overdose in the state spiked by 61 percent between 2003 and 2009. As the Sheriff of Broward County told a reporter, "We have more pain clinics than McDonald's."[1] Greedy, unethical doctors were passing out prescriptions like free water bottles at a disaster site, with fat, happy pharmaceutical companies gladly filling the pipeline. During this period the supply lines spread north into states such as Georgia, Alabama, North and South Carolina, Tennessee, Kentucky, and West Virginia, with Interstate 75 now nicknamed the "Oxy Express." Similar to how cocaine had penetrated all of America once Colombia's drug lords established a base in Miami and South Florida, the Oxy Express brought death and despair to Appalachia in the form of what was dubbed *hillbilly heroin*.

By the time the father of the opiate epidemic, Purdue Pharma, created a gel-form "tamper proof" version of their medicine in 2013, more than seventy tons per year of the addictive pills were being dispensed by US pharmacies. In 2007, Purdue had finally admitted it was guilty of deceptive marketing during legal battles that reached the Supreme Court. The same OxyContin marketed for its first decade as a nonaddictive alternative to other pain meds was indeed highly addictive when crushed and used recreationally, the company acknowledged. The $600 million fine the huge drugmaker was ordered to pay to settle claims against it was a relatively small penalty compared to the billions in profits it has raked in over many years,[2] wealth that landed Purdue's owners in the top twenty of Forbes's 2015 list of America's Richest Families.[3] When considered against the tens of thousands of lives lost and ruined, the penance now seems particularly insufficient.

We knew nothing about this while consumed with our continuing desperate attempts to find and rescue our missing son. Sitting in my SUV on watch outside the looming building that I still sensed would be central to any chance to save Tommy, I reflected on how we could possibly have gotten to this point.

Three years earlier, we had decided to enroll Tommy in a small, private Christian school for eighth grade, concerned with his choice of friends at the public middle school. It seemed like a great fit. With his friendly and gentle personality, he rarely ran afoul of the old-school headmistress, whose dress and demeanor resembled Dana Carvey's SNL character "church lady." A strict disciplinarian, she patrolled the school halls and was known to pull out a ruler and dole out demerits for things like a boy's hair barely touching his collar or a girl's skirt being one-eighth of an inch too short.

At the school, Tommy got involved in the soccer program, which he loved. As in his earlier club experience, he became the team's underdog—well liked by teammates, although not a particularly hard worker, and the one everyone screamed for to score when he had the chance to get on the field during a lopsided game. Unfortunately, soccer was one of the only sports the tiny school was competitive at, and at the JV level he was one of only two kids cut. This seemed to crush what little self-esteem he had left. He would have been happy to be a team manager on that team, handing out towels or water during breaks, anything to feel part of the group. Unfortunately, the type of self-absorbed, overcompetitive men that dominate most youth sports decided he lacked the talent and work ethic to be worthy of their coaching.

When I protested via email to the athletic director, I received the kind of holier-than-thou response that sometimes gives Christians a bad reputation. Apparently winning was more important than acceptance, and the way the whole thing was handled seemed very counter to the biblical principles for which the school stood.

For Tommy, even though competitive rowing later entered the picture for a period of time, this rejection coincided with the beginning of his slide. Coming home to an empty house every day after school while his parents shuttled his three siblings around to a myriad of sports and activities may have made him feel lonely and worthless. Sitting in hospital or recovery center waiting rooms years later, I'd often lament how it must have made him feel when his exuberant father and brothers came bounding into the room after an exciting sports contest, the father often wearing the coach uniform. Tommy had tried to find an activity where he could earn the type of praise two brothers and a sister received from a home run, touchdown, or winning performance but had often fallen short. Now he spent hours alone while the rest of his family were at the field, gym, or auditorium.

Oblivious to this then, I later realized that the most important thing Mary or I could ever give any of our kids was our time and focused attention. Nothing was more important to each of them than this. No new electronic gadget, toy, or game came close to their need for time together to talk, laugh, or simply admire the clouds in silence, time when one or both of us were present and not glued to the television or the latest texts or emails on our phones. Focused attention that let each one of them know they were our number-one priority, providing the affirmation and love that is essential to building positive self-esteem. Tommy frequently was short-changed when it came to such time and attention.

"Don't forget to stop and smell the roses," my aging mother, born and raised during the Great Depression, would often urge during our phone calls. "Enjoy your children; they'll be gone before you know it."

Too caught up in the daily whirlwind of life, I mostly ignored her advice. Even when with my children physically, I was not always truly present emotionally. Caught up in my own thoughts and worries, often triggered by the incessant jolts delivered by my shock collar, aka cell phone, I often did not truly connect in a way that let them know I was listening intently or accepting what they had to say. Kids definitely know the difference.

Tommy eventually got a job working at a local sandwich shop, which seemed to lift his spirits and provide a sense of belonging. As it turns out, an older teen who worked at the store was supplying many of his younger coworkers with marijuana. Since this person lived less than two blocks away, employees apparently walked to his apartment to get high during their fifteen-minute breaks. We later learned, among other deceits, that Tommy sometimes requested we drop him off at work hours before his shift. He would then head to the older teen's place to smoke and hang out before clocking in. Sometimes he would pull the ruse after work, telling us to pick him up two hours after he'd clocked out. With no school activities or sports to occupy his time, our bored and depressed son began turning more and more toward drugs and the temporary escape they provided.

My own feelings of rejection from my loner father led me to initially blame myself for not being a better father to my struggling son. The twelve-step gurus can talk about the three Cs all day long—I didn't Cause it, I can't Control it, and I can't Cure it—but to me the first C was the hardest to swallow. Despite pleas from my other children, wife, friends, and therapist not to blame myself, the pain I felt over feeling that I'd failed Tommy reopened many of the childhood wounds I'd worked hard to overcome.

Like most sons, I longed to spend time with my dad. Unfortunately, most of the very little time he offered when I was a child was spent clearing brush, delivering firewood, or other chores. Desperate for his acceptance, I tried to keep up with this quick-tempered, physically imposing man, often getting yelled at for not being fast enough, strong enough, or skilled enough for the tasks at hand. When it came to the fun father-son activities that I longed to share with him, such as fishing or sports, my father almost always preferred to be alone.

Not by intention but due to the simple reality of having brought three sons into the world in less than four years and a daughter a few years later, there simply was not enough time to go around. Despite my best efforts, my gentle-natured, sensitive son who needed affirmation the most was short-changed on the most important thing every boy needs and desires: attention and acceptance from his father.

As I was handing out the flyers with Tommy's image, I wondered if we'd ever find him. *Would the last time he would ever hear my voice be the night I yelled at him over the disguised Coke can?* Around this time, Mary visited the police station in the city where we lived and entered Tommy into the missing persons database. I brought a flyer into a CVS store in the area of Orlando we'd been searching, and the manager recognized Tommy. He had seen him the previous night, reaffirming my hunch that he was still in the vicinity. Another flyer was left with an Orlando cop whom I flagged down and unsuccessfully tried to convince to search the abandoned naval building. I took other flyers to the local Greyhound and Amtrak stations, where I learned that any child fourteen or older could buy a ticket to anywhere, no questions asked.

But my thoughts kept returning to the abandoned building, as if a homing beacon planted there kept summoning me back. Mary and my friends insisted that he was likely long gone from the area.

"C'mon, Rick, give it up," Mary said, not hiding her irritation. "You're wasting time you could be spending on searching other areas."

"My gut tells me he's still there," I responded. "Leave me alone and stop telling me what to do!"

I refused to waver from focusing on the dark, imposing building in the center of Orlando's version of Smallville, which I had already entered with Rich two nights earlier and searched alone the previous morning. With my hope waning, the phone rang. It was my eldest son, Paul, who was in college two hours away.

"Dad, I'm on my way; I'll be there within a couple hours," he said.

"No, Paul, please don't come; this is not your problem, and I don't want you to get distracted by this!"

"Dad, he's my brother. I'm coming no matter what you say," he insisted.

By 9:00 p.m. our expanded search team congregated outside the building on a dark, rainy Sunday evening. It now included Paul, a friend he had enlisted, and my friends Kevin and Rich. We set out to do what the police had refused to. We moved through the building's ground floor quietly, carefully stepping over broken glass and straining our ears for any sound or movement from the floors above that might break the eerie silence. Half-expecting someone to jump out at us every time we opened another door or turned a dark corner, we began searching the seemingly endless maze of rooms and potential hiding places. Only our flashlight beams broke the blackness within the windowless basement level.

"Check this out," called Rich from what seemed like a long way away.

"Where are you?" I responded, irritated that his loud voice would warn anyone in the building, including Tommy, of our presence.

As I wound my way through the corridors toward his voice and turned a corner, I could see Rich standing at the opposite corner of the building from where we'd entered. For the past three days and nights we'd focused on what we all had assumed was the only entry point to the structure, but here, as Rich discovered, was yet another gaping hole on the other side of the building. Since the ordeal began, I'd diligently kept watch from the opposite side. Positioning my car at a safe distance, binoculars at the ready, I'd been obsessing on the spot where Rich and I had first gained entry days earlier. From morning coffee through afternoon business calls, I'd been certain Tommy would eventually enter or emerge through that access point. Now we realized that the entire time he could have been entering and leaving from the other direction, outside of our sight zone.

Feeling a little deflated for not more carefully searching the perimeter during daylight hours (tall grass obscured the newly-discovered opening the time we'd walked past it at night), we resumed our search. The crumbling concrete stairwells caused our group to pause and tensions rose, just as they had on previous searches.

"How do we know there isn't a homeless guy waiting to jump us?" Paul asked, gripping his baseball bat tighter.

"Look, let's just get this over with," I said, taking the lead up the stairwell steps to the second floor, every ounce of energy consumed by fighting back my fear.

On the second floor I shone my light into the open elevator shaft and warned the group about this potential hazard, which was repeated in several other places throughout the building. Kevin suggested that we separate into two groups, allowing us to more quickly scour the two wings and two sets of group bathrooms and small rooms on every floor.

Systematically we searched the entire building this way, all the way up to the roof. Nothing. Discouraged and drained, we stepped back out into the light drizzle of the evening and headed our separate ways, barely exchanging a word.

3

HUNCHES AND
HEARTACHES

The peaceful sounds of waves breaking onto the beach and
children laughing were pierced by two words from my wife.

"Where's Tommy?!"

I quickly dropped the book I'd been reading in the beach
bag and scanned the water's edge. My young sons Barry and
Paul were busy digging channels through the sand and using
plastic buckets to fill them with seawater. But five-year-old
Tommy was nowhere to be found. I rushed toward the ocean
instinctively, scanning the breakers and shallows, but there
was no sign of his curly blonde hair and blue bathing suit
with dolphins on it. By now Mary was out of her chair and
in panic mode. What if he went under or got pulled out by
a rip current? What if a stranger convinced him to go for
an ice cream?

Our oceanside vacation in Stone Harbor, New Jersey, was
something we looked forward to every summer. It was one of

47

the few places where we could relax without worrying about one of our three young energetic sons darting in front of a car, falling out of a tree, or tumbling down a flight of stairs. All we had to do was keep them in front of us and not let them go very far into the ocean without us. They would amuse themselves for hours in the surf, sand, and shallow tide pools, making this the perfect place for a young couple to relax with their kids.

Only now one was missing, and we were frantic.

"Have you seen your brother?" Mary asked Paul.

"Yeah, he's right up there." Paul pointed, motioning toward the dunes many yards behind where our chairs were positioned.

In our intense focus on the ocean and its dangers, we hadn't even considered that Tommy could be behind us. But there he was, rolling in the sand just in front of the dunes.

While two of our three young boys preferred the waves and wet sand at the ocean's edge, Tommy loved to cover himself in the hot dry sand at the top of the beach. We found him rolling around contentedly at the hottest part of the day, body and hair completely covered, without a care in the world.

"Hi, Mommy, hi, Daddy," he said with a sweet smile.

The silent terror that now ruled our every thought on the fourth day since Tommy disappeared felt far greater than that brief panic attack on the beach a decade earlier. Mary and I shifted our focus to the growing possibility that he'd left the area completely, and maybe even the state. We contacted the Amtrak police to try to determine if there were any records that he'd boarded a train. Mary decided to reach out to our local police department given the disinterest shown by police in the adjacent city where we'd been searching. She found a detective willing to help, and before long the girl we suspected had been hiding Tommy received a visit. The detective questioned her and searched the premises, including a small shack out back, but found no clues.

Frustrated and not sure what to do next, Mary and I began blaming each other.

"Maybe if you were around more this wouldn't have happened," she said, firing the first volley.

"If you weren't constantly stressing him out with your micromanaging, maybe he wouldn't feel the need to escape," I retaliated.

"Oh, so it's my fault?" she said, her voice rising.

"You're suggesting it's my fault; stop blaming me!" I shouted.

"You're the one that threatened him!"

"As usual, it's never your fault, Mary. Just once I'd love for you to take responsibility for the stress you put on this family with your perfectionism and controlling nature."

"To hell with you, Mr. Perfect," she said, storming off and slamming the door behind her.

This was certainly not the first time we turned on each other under the pressure of our son's behavior and struggles, and it was a pattern that would occur over and over for years. It's a miracle that our marriage survived the finger-pointing and fighting that seemed to arise every time Tommy or another child found trouble or suffered a setback. Despite both of our training in social work and communications, all of this went out the window in an emotional tornado of turmoil when the safety of one of our kids was at stake. Rarely were we on the same page.

Before my anger from our little dustup subsided, the telephone rang. It was a manager from the CVS pharmacy where I'd left a picture of Tommy a day earlier, just a few blocks from the building we'd been searching. Once again, the strong feeling that kept me returning to that area proved correct.

"Your son is in my store right now," he whispered. "Get down here right away!"

"Please call the police and see if they can detain him," I replied, immediately rushing to my car.

By the time I arrived about twenty minutes later, it was already too late. My son, who was likely in the store to steal more over-the-counter drugs to abuse, had sensed the manager watching him. He bolted from the store and sped off on a red bicycle, the manager told me. The police had already come and gone, fairly disinterested in the situation as usual.

Now days into the search and exhausted from lack of sleep, my adrenaline kicked in, and I became desperate. I simply had to find him and do so quickly. After a quick phone call, our friends Rich and Cherie showed up in separate cars to help us patrol the area and stake out the building. Paul loaded two bicycles into his borrowed vehicle and met me. Mary came in her own car.

We devised a plan to take full advantage of our expanded resources. From the beginning, we knew Tommy had been spending time with his friend John who lived in the neighborhood. On the first night we'd rung the doorbell of his house and spoken with his father outside. Essentially the teen was a stranger to his own parents, who kept their bedroom door locked at all times to protect the valuables and prescription medicines inside. Their son was rarely seen on weekends, and even during the week, his father said, his presence was mostly noted by the pizza boxes or dirty dishes left behind from late-night or daytime visits. He had already been in and out of rehab programs and kicked out of school, and he was allowed to still have a key only because authorities had advised that they could face charges of abandonment should they kick him out prior to his eighteenth birthday.

In essence, his battle-weary parents had thrown in the towel on their only child. At the time, I recall being very sad and somewhat disgusted at their attitude. Two years later, well into our own fight to survive the hell of having an addict child, I completely sympathized. However, there was no way we were going to quit.

Luckily, the father had given me his cell number at our initial meeting, so I called him at work, reminded him who I was, and explained the situation.

"We haven't seen our son in three days," he said.

"Does he have a bike?" I asked.

"Yes."

"What color is it?"

"Red," he replied. "It's in the garage."

I immediately assumed that this was the bike mentioned by the drugstore manager and that Tommy would be at his friend's home. Less than an hour after the initial call alerting us that our son, identified by the flyer, had been at CVS, I found myself again on the doorstep of this teen. Tired, frustrated, and angry, I was ready to intimidate his friend into giving me some answers and break down the door if needed to find my son. Paul had a better and wiser plan.

"Dad, you're too worked up, let me talk to him," Paul said. "He's scared, but maybe he will talk to me."

Paul rang the bell and the teen let him inside. At the back, garage side of the connected townhouses, Rich staked out the alley in case Tommy was inside and tried to slip out that way.

After what seemed like an eternity, Paul emerged from the house and walked slowly to the car.

"Tommy's not there," Paul said. "The kid says he hasn't seen him since last Friday, but I think he's lying. He's really sketchy."

"Did you search the entire place to make sure he wasn't hiding?"

"No, he wouldn't let me," Paul said. "Do you want me to go back in and force him?"

"No," I said. "The last thing we need is you getting in trouble over this."

We again called the police. Finally the responding officers seemed responsive to our plight and ready to help. They entered and searched the entire dwelling, except for the locked master bedroom and the garage that for some strange reason they skipped, but found no one. When they came out we begged them to go back one more time to at least determine the whereabouts of the red bike. Indeed, there was a red bike in the garage, as the father had said, but it was covered in cobwebs with two flat tires. Clearly this was not the one we were looking for. We'd jumped to a false conclusion. Once again, we found ourselves with no clues about where our son might be.

With no other real options available, all of us in the area, and unwilling to give up, we kept pushing. Rich and I jumped onto bicycles to search the paved bike trails that wound around the lake and through sections of the woods where we'd heard homeless encampments were located. Taking different routes, we rode in search of red bikes, showing Tommy's picture to those we came across.

Coming up empty, we returned to the group and in our own vehicles staked out both sides of Tommy's friend's home as well as the abandoned building we had searched. Trying to keep a distance, we hoped that eventually the friend would emerge and lead us to Tommy.

Paul had pegged it. *Sketchy* was the perfect term for this guy. He'd emerge from the front door on foot, nervously look around, and then walk a block or two down an alley before turning around and coming back. Fifteen minutes later the garage door would open and he'd take off on a black bicycle, only to return within minutes. Keeping the heat on this confused and obviously drugged-up kid, we hoped that he'd either crack and tell us where Tommy was or lead us right to him.

This cat-and-mouse game went on for the entire afternoon, and at one point my friend Rich, sporting a thick mustache and driving a very undercover-cop-like dark Chevy Caprice, rolled down his window to talk to him as he walked by.

"Look, we don't care about you or getting you in trouble," Rich told him. "We just want Tommy, and then we'll leave you alone. But until then, you won't be able to wipe your butt without one of us being there."

Then, from my familiar post watching the abandoned building, I couldn't believe my eyes. A group of four young men ducked through the fallen section of chain link fence and ambled across the overgrown lot toward the opening through which Rich and I had first entered the building. One of them walked, dressed, and from a distance looked like Tommy. I wasn't able to get the binoculars on them before they stepped into the darkness of the building, but my hope rose that the nightmare would soon be over.

I called the officer that had been helpful earlier, and he promised to investigate. A call from Cherie reported a couple kids running from the back of the building, dashing my hopes. Shortly after that I saw the officer enter the building, and then emerge a few minutes later with the four in tow. Unfortunately, Tommy was not among them.

The anguish we felt as parents trying to locate a missing child in danger was unlike anything either my wife or I had ever experienced. Despite both of us having been through a disproportionate share of trauma in our lives, the intense heartache and dread were unbearable. The root of this pain also likely made me leap to the conclusion that it was Tommy I saw among the four kids entering the sinister building that afternoon when it wasn't.

With the emotional roller-coaster ride continuing and the day's light fading quickly, Paul called me with a new plan.

"I talked to John again," he said. "He's getting really wigged out by being followed and is very nervous. He said some old dude with a mustache is particularly creeping him out," referring to Rich, sparking a brief, tension-relieving chuckle between us.

"Let me go alone and convince him to show me where he and Tommy hang out when they go to the building," Paul suggested.

"I don't know, son. It sounds dangerous, and I'm afraid he'll just lead you on a wild-goose chase."

"Let me try, we've got nothing to lose."

Before long, from my regular observation post, pride mixed with hope as I watched Tommy's friend emerge from Paul's car. The pair then walked across the lot and entered the building.

During what seemed like an eternity, I reflected on the man our eldest son was becoming. Paul had the unfortunate luck to be the firstborn of a damaged father and flawed mother, both products of difficult childhoods marred by divorce and dysfunction.

Paul was challenging from the day he was born after twenty-three hours of labor. As a baby he wouldn't sleep and cried constantly. His ear infections were frequent, and he had a double-hernia operation at age two. Once he could crawl, there was no stopping his climbing, running, and chattering. He had three trips to the emergency room for multiple stitches before his fifth birthday, two a testament to his climbing coupled with the unforgiving nature of the old cast-iron radiators in our century-old house. It almost seemed like he enjoyed smashing his head against those things! By the time I'd make it home from Manhattan to the emergency room, the crisis would already be over, Mary's blood-soaked blouse the reminder of what I'd missed.

Clearly, Paul was very intelligent and full of energy, but his motor was always racing full speed. We enjoyed great times together at places such as the Bronx Zoo and Yankee Stadium. Tommy came along nineteen months later, then Barry twenty months after that. With Paul on the smaller side, Tommy average size, and Barry a bit taller, the three boys were virtually the same height, and frequently we were asked if they were triplets. Particularly after Barry was born, and we became outnumbered, life became more challenging. Mary took a hiatus from her career to focus on the kids after Tommy was born when we realized that given the costs of child care, commuting, and dry cleaning, she'd be going to a job in the city to bring in less than $10,000 per year.

We enjoyed our Stone Harbor vacations on the southern Jersey Shore and often spent weekends with friends and their children, celebrating many birthday parties, communion celebrations, and other events with large groups of family and friends. Life was good with one small but not insignificant problem. I was rarely home.

Still chasing the recognition and affirmation that my father had never provided, I was absolutely driven in my career as a journalist, determined to make a name for myself. My first job in Manhattan, paying just $11,500 a year, earned me the spoils of a cockroach-infested basement apartment in Queens with no phone, no television, a college-sized refrigerator, and a stoop-over handheld shower hose over a makeshift metal drain. I had to walk four blocks to the nearest phone booth to put in a collect call to my fiancée, Mary, who was living with her grandparents in the Bronx.

Before long I had a better job, for $500 more a year, and over the next few years continued to work hard and ascend in my career. By the time we had our three boys, I was leading a national magazine and traveling across the nation, and occasionally to Europe, to spread the magazine's goodwill. I loved every moment with my sons; however, I wasn't home enough to have enough of them.

The real wake-up call that changed the course of our lives came out of the mouth of Paul, then five, who while frolicking on a playground pointed up at an airplane flying overhead and asked, "Daddy, is that where you live?"

As much a knife to the heart as his words felt like that day, it didn't really hit me until the next week while on a flight to the West Coast. Trying to hide my face from the passenger next to me, I broke down sobbing. For the first time I realized that I'd created a different version of how my own father lived his life—for himself, not his sons. As much as I paid lip service to being a great dad, and as much love as I had for each son, how I spent my time proved they were not truly my first priority. Even when in town, there were many long days when I left to catch the train before they awoke and returned home after they were tucked in at night. While my own confidence and self-actualization had materialized, it came at a cost to my kids. Deciding to change course before it was too late, I began listening to headhunter calls and considering new opportunities.

It was particularly difficult to tell my mentor and boss Jim Doherty about my decision when the right opportunity came along. Jim, a successful businessman who I sensed had certain regrets about his own years as a father, may have seen me as somewhat of a second chance given the age difference between us. "Van Warner is a work in progress," he'd frequently tell people, just as my first mentor, my high school football coach John Pilato, had. Jim taught me about business, which I was essentially clueless about having grown up in the household of a teacher and a jack-of-all-trades high school dropout. With his career as a successful restaurant executive drawing to a close, Jim had been convinced by my then employer to move to the opposite coast and turn our business around. He plucked me out of a team of older, more experienced colleagues as his right-hand guy to make this happen. A hard-nosed Irishman, Jim wasn't one to mince words and certainly was not a particularly sensitive man, instead cut from the cloth of World War II warriors raised by the notion that real men don't cry.

On a train home from Washington one day I got a call from my boss that both he and his boss had been fired that day and that Jim wanted to see me early the next morning.

57

I walked into his office not knowing whether I would be fired or promoted. As I entered, Jim was pacing furiously, smoking a cigarette. He was obviously agitated and spoke in short, direct bursts at whoever was on the other end of his phone. He motioned for me to be seated, cut his call short, and began to speak.

"OK, Van Warner, you might've heard that both guys above you aren't here anymore," he growled, taking a pull off his smoke. "I didn't come here from LA to be third place or in the red. We should be the top business in the market, and I plan to get us there. I don't give a damn what it takes."

Still uncertain about my fate, I nodded.

"I see something in you that you don't see in yourself, so I'm going to give you a shot," he said. "This is big for you if you grab the brass ring. I'm going to give you six months to see what you can do. I'll give you a lot of rope, got no time to babysit. What you do with that rope is up to you. You can either climb it, and I'll promote you to editor and give you the money that goes with it. Or," he said with a piercing smirk that I later came to secretly enjoy, especially if he was using it on others, "you can tie a noose and hang yourself! It's up to you. Whaddaya say?"

From that day forward I was all in, gladly accepting Jim's coaching and guidance, the second major mentor in my life to compensate for an absentee father. I made the most of this opportunity and learned much about both business and life, and the years we spent together were the most rewarding and fun times of my career. Together our team did return our magazine to the top and the perks included getting to know self-made restaurant industry legends such as Dave Thomas, Norm Brinker, Joe Lee, and Carl Karcher. It meant spending time with rising chefs before chefs became celebrities, talented and eccentric people including Wolfgang Puck, Emeril Lagasse, Charlie Palmer, Rick Bayless, and many others. We were treated like royalty at the finest restaurants and resorts throughout the nation. It was a far cry from how I'd grown up, where the rare visit to a restaurant usually consisted of a Carroll's fast-food drive-through or Ponderosa buffet line.

Despite how much I enjoyed my role and the tremendous love I had for my editorial team, mentors, and job, Paul's innocent words suggesting he didn't even realize we lived under the same roof continued to haunt me. They reminded me of the dejected feeling I'd get every morning during my childhood summers, running to the lake's edge after waking only to see that my dad's boat hoist was empty. He left at dawn every day to go fishing, never offering to let me tag along. I was determined to break that cycle, and within a few months, Mary and I packed our three young boys and two springer spaniels into the minivan and began the long drive to start a new life in Florida.

As he had on the playground fifteen years earlier, Paul once again had galvanized our actions with a new approach as the draining search for Tommy continued. Just fifteen minutes after Paul and Tommy's nervous friend whom we'd been stalking entered the abandoned building, my cell phone rang.

"I've got him," Paul said.

"Will he come out?" I asked.

"He's tripping balls," Paul said. "Give me time."

An agonizing thirty minutes later, and several days after Tommy had disappeared, Paul emerged from the building walking slowly, his arm draped across Tommy's shoulders.

John walked a couple steps behind. What Paul had mistaken for a hallucinogenic trip on LSD or mushrooms was actually Tommy on Oxy pills, enough to have put him into the zombie-like haze we found him in.

By now, Mary had returned with our youngest son, Barry. Also on hand were the Orlando police officer who had to remove Tommy from the missing persons database for us to legally leave with him and the helpful detective from our local police department.

The tears flowed as we hugged Tommy and told him how much we missed and loved him. Looking dazed and somewhat blinded by the setting sun's light, he showed little emotion, yet I sensed he was relieved.

"I love you," he said in a weak, faint voice.

Within hours Tommy was safely ensconced in a hospital psychiatric facility for detoxification. Our search was finally over, but the journey was just beginning.

4

COPING WITH CHAOS

The hustle and bustle of the new school year had a special significance that fall, if you could even consider it autumn given the relentless heat and humidity in Florida during September. Tommy was reentering high school for his senior year, a fresh chance to leave his chemical demons behind and move on with his life.

Jessie and I arrived at her middle school for orientation. The past nine months had been particularly difficult, not just because of Tommy's continuing struggles but also due to a sudden illness in our family.

On the day of the previous Christmas Eve, Mary and I were summoned to her doctor's office for a consultation. The doctor delivered the bad news. The lump in her breast was indeed cancer, and she would require surgery as soon as possible. Merry Christmas!

We decided to wait until the afternoon of Christmas Day to sit down with our three sons to share what was happening. We told our young daughter later and in a different way.

Whether or not Mary's diagnosis impacted or triggered our most sensitive son's rapid descent into full-fledged opiate addiction is something we'll never know. It certainly cannot have helped. During this period he was already smoking a lot of marijuana, and we suspected he was using other drugs. We continued to uncover hidden pipes made of pens and empty sockets, as well as bongs made from plastic water bottles. We had shifted from being parents into being detectives. We became obsessed with stopping his behavior and ensuring he was keeping his word when he denied using. Urine drug tests from Walgreen's, seemingly a profitable product given the high price of the kits and pervasiveness of the problem, became a staple in our home. In ill-fated attempts at deterrence, we would require a surprise test on any of our sons at a moment's notice, particularly Tommy.

"Where have you been, son?" I asked him one night when his huge black pupils seemed to be blotting out way too much of his corneas.

"At Austin's house playing video games," he lied.

"Time for a drug test; you know the drill."

"Really, Dad? This is stupid, but it's your money."

He complied, but not really. Much later we learned that Tommy was beating the tests by keeping a medicine dropper full of bleach, easily obtainable from our laundry room, in his bathroom at all times. Even when I walked into the room behind him to observe him peeing into the sample cup, he deftly would slide the dropper up into the long sleeve of the shirts he always wore and then squeeze its contents into the cup along with his urine stream. Opting to stand behind him rather than stare at his genitals while he filled the pee cup, I never noticed this clever trick and would have never known about it had Tommy not confessed it during one of his recovery attempts.

Meanwhile, we continued to ratchet down the screws on his social life each time we caught him doing something wrong, which was frequently. A particularly low point occurred when I received a call from a close friend on the morning after our family had attended a small social gathering at his home. Their son, a few years younger than Tommy, woke up to find most of the money in his piggy bank missing, and he suspected Tommy. I told my friend that I'd check and call him back, then marched down to Tommy's room with dread. I woke him up and confronted him.

"Did you steal money out of Bruce's room last night?"

"No, why?"

"Don't lie to me, did you take money or not?"

"Yeah."

"Where is it?"

"Here," he said, sliding open a drawer to reveal the exact amount missing.

"What is wrong with you? What were you thinking?"

"I don't know. I needed money and didn't think he'd miss it."

"You mean you thought you could get away with it, right?"

"I guess."

"How many times have we talked about the importance of always being honest, never stealing, and respecting other people's stuff?" I asked. "If there is anything I can't stand, it's lying, cheating, and stealing. Lately you've been doing all three. What is going on with you? What is it you need so badly that you would steal for?"

"Sorry, I made a mistake."

"Get your butt out of bed and get dressed. We're heading over to Bruce's house so you can return the money and apologize."

Bruce and his parents accepted the apology and money with great grace, going out of their way to diffuse the awkwardness of the situation.

"He's a good kid who just made a mistake," Bruce's father said. "Hopefully, he'll learn from this." Sadly, he didn't.

The embarrassing visit was the first of many times Tommy's problem would strain friendships, regardless of the kindness and understanding usually shown at first. I didn't blame anyone for not trusting him and not wanting a teenager who would rob a younger kid's piggy bank in their home. Over time this added to Tommy's isolation, as we became hesitant to even put him in such situations. Much later we'd adopt more of a bunker mentality, becoming defensive or resentful toward friends who seemed to look at Tommy the wrong way or make a careless comment. *Unless you've walked in our shoes*, we'd think, *who are you to judge?* Today we recognize that everyone has personal challenges in their lives, whether they choose to share them or not, and have developed thicker skin, especially when it comes to our children.

Although the telltale signs of drug abuse were there, particularly stealing and lying, we figured we were dealing with the usual teenage rebellion and not a descent into hard drug addiction. We took away his teenage lifelines, the cell phone and the car, and essentially had him at a point just short of house arrest.

Recognizing that his self-esteem was likely the core of the problem—he was acting out to escape from internal pain—

we connected him with a renowned local therapist. Beginning a pattern that would repeat itself over the next two years, it seemed to be working for the first couple of weeks.

In uncommon wisdom for a young man who had suffered and overcome many tough issues himself—substance abuse, thankfully, not among them—our eldest son, Paul, offered this perspective during one of our countless moments of despair: "You have to decide what the most important boundaries are, make him sign a contract on those, then let him start fresh," Paul advised. "He's been grounded for so long now that he can't see any way out. He just wants to live like a normal kid, going out with friends. He's ready to give up."

Given the hindsight of the hell yet to come, we probably should have listened. None of us can turn back the clocks to know what might have changed, if anything, and dwelling on past regrets is as unproductive as obsessing about the future. But within days of Paul's warning, Tommy had again vanished.

Walking hand-in-hand with Jessie into her new school in September, I somehow felt fresh hope. Following two successful surgeries in early January and a few months of exhausting radiation treatments, Mary was back to her usual whirlwind self as three of our four children adjusted to the end of sleeping in during the summer and resuming the routine of early morning classes.

For ten-year-old Jessie, the end of summer included a sparkling new school to explore. This, the first of her middle school years, would be spent in a modern building next to and towering over the old dark-brick neighborhood elementary school where she'd spent the previous six seasons of learning.

Jessie had mixed feelings about the change.

"I don't like it, Daddy," she said with a sigh. "I miss my old school."

Change can be a difficult thing, particularly for a girl who had witnessed far more than her share of strife during her brief ten years on the planet. As we wandered the halls exchanging greetings with friends and teachers, her apprehension disappeared, and within minutes she was dutifully labeling her school supplies, signing her name to every item. As we completed our rounds, her nostalgia returned.

"Can we visit my old teacher?" Jessie asked. "Pleeaase!"

As we walked hand-in-hand down the sidewalk from new to old school, my daughter's mood brightened noticeably. The warm hug she gave last year's teacher spoke to her yearning for stability, familiarity, and the known versus unknown.

A few miles away our youngest son, Barry, also embarked on a new beginning, but one mostly lost in the chaos of our current family life. As a tenth-grader he stepped into classes on the big high school campus for the first time, walking the halls Tommy had walked before and would very briefly walk again. Shouldering a stigma created by his older brother, tempered by his success as an athlete, he rubbed the sleep from his eyes and persevered, just as he always seemed to.

For Tommy, the conversations about fresh chances and new beginnings had apparently fallen on deaf ears. His mind clouded by the substance he had snorted that morning, he wandered the halls reconnecting with old friends and aimlessly drifted from class to class without taking a single note in his planner.

By now, making money at his restaurant job and trying to find a way to get his own apartment were the primary things on his mind. His sights were set on getting out as quickly as possible. With the drug-retarded judgment of a twelve-year-old, the high school senior was certain that he could make a go of it on his own, free from the restrictions of a temperamental father and controlling mother.

"I'm saving up for an apartment," he said several times. "It's time for me to go out on my own. You don't want me here, and I don't want to be here."

"Son, do you have any idea how much it costs to rent an apartment? You're still in high school; this is silly."

"It's my life, you can't tell me what to do."

"Until you're eighteen, you are our responsibility, and we have the legal right to insist you live by our rules."

"That's why I need to get out of here," he said, deploying the familiar circular and manipulative logic we grew to understand was closely tied to his level of drug use. "You won't let me do what I want here, so I need to move on."

"Where do you think you'll get the money for two months' rent up front, working at the restaurant?"

"I'll figure it out."

"Sure you will."

The illusion of Tommy successfully completing high school while living at home was short-lived. We could never have imagined then how many times the scenario about to take place would repeat itself. Our son's return to opiate use engulfed our entire family and created a lingering fog of tension that surrounded every waking moment. As usual, my wife and I continued to disagree over what to do.

At meetings of Nar-Anon, a support group for the families of addicts, we had heard about the madness and manipulation that addicts desperate for a fix resort to. Yet neither Mary nor I fully recognized how much it consumed both of us and negatively impacted our other children until much later. Between Tommy's behavior and our desperate attempts to change it, our son's addiction sucked up nearly 100 percent of the entire family's energy.

One of our toughest challenges was trying to fall asleep at night worrying that the call would finally come that our beautiful, loving second son was dead or in jail. In time we would actually pray for the latter option, since it seemed the only one that involved him being alive and not able to use drugs. Sadly, not even jail stopped the drug use, as we later learned.

Every time the phone rang our hearts sank, certain that it was the police or a friend with bad news to report. Tommy was like a ghost that summer, appearing occasionally but vanishing again just as quickly. When his whereabouts were unknown, the familiar bickering between Mary and me would return.

"How can you sleep knowing he's out there?" she demanded.

"I'm over this, we have to let him go," I replied.

"What do you mean let him go, just let him die?"

"There's nothing we can do, and we cannot go on like this. The stress is unbearable! I'm convinced it had a lot to do with your cancer."

"He's my baby, and I don't care what you do, but I'm not giving up."

"I didn't say give up, I said we have to focus on our other children right now. Everyone is suffering."

"They're fine, it's you that needs to change. You're eating and drinking way too much."

"Oh, so now it's about me, what a surprise. You just love to blame others but never look in the mirror on how much stress you create by trying to control every little thing any of us do."

"So it's my fault Tommy's messed up; I'm the one that drove him away!"

"That's not what I'm saying—"

"That's fine," she interrupted, "go pour yourself another drink."

There were times we wondered if our then twenty-five-year marriage would survive the utter desperation we endured on a daily basis. We would also sometimes find ourselves swapping roles, similar to a good cop, bad cop scenario.

Mary would go through a period of smothering Tommy with love while at the same time trying to control or track his every movement. I had reached a point of resenting his presence. It took me months to overcome this anger and resentment and shift toward forgiveness. Years earlier I'd shown up on my father's doorstep to forgive him for all he had put me, my mother, and my siblings through, and I was overcome with the peace and happiness that God granted me through this simple act. But it took considerable prayer and the encouragement of new friends in a small weekly men's group to thaw the hardness that had engulfed my heart. Forgiveness and acceptance, the pillars of faith in Christ, were instrumental in our family's sanity and survival through the madness of Tommy's addiction. But it took years to truly get there.

Rarely were Mary and I on the same page at the same time. Every time she was ready to offer another chance, I'd be ready to shut the door, and vice versa. We would continue this pattern for years, through countless battles and dangerous rescue attempts to save our son, before we finally were able to become unified in our resolve to never give up. Although we remain somewhat divided regarding how we choose to practice our faith, we are stronger and more united than ever as parents and life partners.

One of the most difficult lessons a family of an opiate addict on the hamster wheel of destruction must learn is that the person they love has absolutely no regard for the impact their behavior has on those around them. They may appear pretty much the same, and even now and then show glimpses of the person they once were, but only one thing dominates their every thought—the next high.

Having come of age in the '70s, neither Mary nor I were strangers to smoking pot or dabbling with other substances. The idea that the wacky weed was a gateway drug had always seemed silly and simplistic to me, and I'd long believed that alcohol was far more damaging to the human body. Apparently my late father, Dick, reluctantly agreed with this view.

"How could you do this to Mom and Dad," I had self-righteously demanded of my older sister when she was caught with a bag of pot at sixteen, something she has since reminded and teased me about. Over my mother's ranting and crying, I can still clearly recall my father's take. "The biggest problem I have is that it's illegal," he said.

Much later in life, having won his battle with alcoholism without ever attending a single meeting of Alcoholics Anonymous, my father told me the story of his late-life encounter with marijuana when he joined a younger couple at their home for Thanksgiving. The saddest days for a man like him who had sobered up too late and already lost his family must have been spending holidays alone. This particular Thanksgiving, my father said his friends kept disappearing into the bathroom together for short periods. Perplexed, he decided he'd had enough.

"Hey, why do you two keep going in there," Dick demanded. "Are you trying to hide something from me? Just be honest, you don't have to hide anything from me."

Knowing that the gig was up, Sally said, "I'm sorry, Dick, we just didn't want to offend you. We're just smoking a little pot."

"Well, hell!" Dick replied. "I might as well try some."

So at sixty-five years old, he got high for the one and only time in his life. He didn't care for the experience.

"I didn't like it," he told me years later. "When I have a cigarette, it's my cigarette. I don't like the idea of someone else's lips being on it. Plus, it made me go right to sleep."

On the rare occasions that one or more of his three children were able to visit my father around a holiday, it was typically for an hour or two at most. For one thing, none of us cared to be in a house where cigarette smoke constantly filled the air and over time managed to turn everything, from furniture fabrics to curtains, a putrid shade of yellow.

My wife and I now chuckle about the first time we took our eldest son to meet him when Paul was just two. With Paul toddling toward him, my father put his lit cigarette in between his lips, and then stretched out his arms to pull him up to his lap.

"Dad," I exclaimed, "put the cigarette down first!"

These brief visits, alone or with members of my own family, were the most conflictive experiences of my life. On the one hand, I felt sorry for the old man and down deep still loved him. On the other, I detested this imposing monster who had berated his family, womanized openly, and treated my mother so poorly. Guilt would drive me to his doorstep, and then anger would make me want to leave again, almost from the second I stepped inside.

Childhood experiences with my father also had given me nasty glimpses of addiction; the hell we were now mired in because of Tommy made its destructive power crystal clear. Whether it is an addict's drug of choice or whatever they can put their hands on, their desire to get high trumps everything else. To satisfy this overpowering need, the addict will manipulate and take advantage of anyone they encounter, regardless of whether that person is a close friend, family member, or stranger. They will lie and steal and even prostitute themselves as a means to that one and only consuming end—to snort, smoke, or shoot up.

Tommy's worsening condition was particularly tough for our cheerful ten-year-old to grasp, especially because the person using was her favorite brother with whom she always shared a special bond. He was the one of her three siblings who had always treated her with the most kindness. Among the many painful things we endured during that first summer of denial was the devastating impact on our young daughter.

"What's wrong with him, Daddy?" Jessie would ask. "Is he going to get better? Does he not like me anymore? Did I do something wrong? Is he going to die?"

These questions only scratch the surface of the confusion our daughter experienced that awful summer, just a few months after dealing with the fear of losing her mother to cancer. Having watched her mom complete radiation therapy, this bubbly and beautiful little princess began to change. Her wonderful, positive view of the world was ripped from her, and she learned far too early that life is fragile and that even the people you love the most might be taken away suddenly.

The manifestations of these changes in perspective were small. And sadly in the chaos that was siphoning every ounce of our energy and focus, at first we missed the signs. Candy wrappers tucked behind the couch. Sassy comments made toward her mom. Awkward comments of concern expressed from friends over her insatiable appetite. Before long, occasional temper outbursts were added to the mix. Indeed, the addiction our son struggled with hurt every one of us as we fought to cope with the dark forces that had swallowed our family.

All this led to an escalating conflict between the mother who gave birth to the stranger now residing in our home and myself. Neither of us was ever going to give up on our son; however, we each coped with the madness differently. The only thing we did agree on was that we were rapidly reaching the point where the needs of our other children, not to mention ourselves, could no longer take a backseat to the problem sucking all the air out of our home.

5

FIGHTING INSIDE AND OUT

Her words were heartbreaking, and I could relate to them on many different fronts. "I felt worthless, like a piece of garbage," the twenty-year-old girl said. "I didn't care if I died, or about my family, or about anything. All I cared about was making sure I could get high."

The speaker was now sober and sharing her past with a group of anxious parents hanging on to every word. The daughter of one of our fellow Nar-Anon support group attendees, she was our guest speaker. The young woman's testimony hit us squarely between the eyes. It was exactly how our son must still feel, we thought. How can we possibly help someone who doesn't want to be helped?

Perhaps the most difficult part of being an addict's parent is accepting that you cannot control or change that person or their actions regardless of how much time, effort, or money you devote to the effort. Twelve-step programs state that the first step toward sobriety for an addict is admitting that they are powerless over their addiction. Nar-Anon doctrine similarly teaches that the first step toward becoming a healthy spouse or parent of an addict is admitting that you can only control yourself.

"I didn't Cause it, I can't Control it, and I can't Cure it," as the doctrine goes. It's a tough concept for most of us to swallow. From the time our babies are born, we parents do everything possible to protect them from the bad in the world. Accepting that we can no longer save our own child is maddening.

After nearly three years and tens of thousands of dollars worth of chasing and rescuing our son, all to no avail, I'd finally accepted that we had no control over him or his behavior. I also now understood that we couldn't change Tommy. But it was the first of the Cs that still tortured my innermost thoughts, that somehow I'd caused the root problem.

There were several things I beat myself up over, wishing life gave us second chances. Having three sons in four years was probably not our smartest decision, particularly given the depth of our own personal struggles and upbringings. Of course, there was no turning back after the most miraculous four days of my life, the birth of each child.

Looking back at the whirlwind of those earlier years, I wish I'd spent more time and focus on Tommy and less time on the sports of my other sons. I regret the number of weekend nights we chose to go out to dinner or events with other couples in lieu of family nights at home playing games. We also could have been more discreet about enjoying wine, beer, or other drinks in our home or at friends' homes during holidays, football games, or simple gatherings.

Despite these regrets and the obvious guilt over the genes I passed on to my son, I've also come to understand that we did not cause his problems. Addiction is an equal-opportunity problem. Addicts come from households of teetotalers and households with gold-standard parenting, if there is such a thing. They are raised in rich neighborhoods and poor neighborhoods, by parents of all colors, shapes, and backgrounds. Addicts come from households like ours, with two parents doing the best they can.

When we allowed Tommy to move home again, after another failed detox and recovery attempt, things at first were peaceful.

"We're so glad to have you back home," Mary said. "Are you hungry, would you like me to make you something?"

"No, I'm good."

We made him sign a contract spelling out the conditions of him being allowed to live with us. It included a strict curfew, pitching in with household chores, and, of course, no drugs.

His return marked yet another role reversal compared to the previous time he had lived under our roof. Having spent the past few months in Nar-Anon and reading several books on the subject, Mary now adopted a firm, tough love approach rather than trying to push him back toward her view of a normal path for a late teen. Clearly relieved that Tommy had survived the streets and brushes with death, she nurtured him to make sure he knew how much he was loved. But she also followed the clear boundaries outlined in the contract and was very conscious not to enable him.

While I understood these concepts, I tried a different approach this time. Instead of my prior "follow our rules or get out" stance, I adopted a more compassionate, nurturing approach at the suggestion of my therapist. Overpowered by my emotional guilt and childhood scars, I had neared the edge of an emotional breakdown. More than ever before, I drank and ate to calm my mind and mute my secret pain. I simply couldn't shake the nagging guilt over having spent more time with Tommy's sports-minded brothers than him, feeling that I'd emotionally abandoned him much like my father had abandoned me. Whether it was Boy Scout campouts or crew meets, I'd missed out on Tommy's activities in lieu of coaching my other sons' teams or following my own musical passions. My inflated pride in my youngest son's various athletic accomplishments didn't help, and I'm certain it must have hurt Tommy to hear me regularly boasting about his little brother.

I was drawn at this time to a restaurant industry leader who was smart, kind, and confident in his faith in Christ. Kim carried himself in a completely different way than the holier-than-thou, arrogant believers that had pushed me away from my faith. He was humble and let his actions speak for his beliefs. I know now that God put Kim in my life to help me discover my purpose, but at first, I just enjoyed being around one of the smartest and kindest people I've ever met. We met for weekly breakfasts to share personal struggles, completed the *Man in the Mirror* book together, and have remained close despite not seeing each other as often. More than anyone else, Kim helped to restore my faith through this brokenhearted and guilt-ridden time.

Meanwhile, I tried to reconnect with my son in a more gentle way. Clearly he was fragile, both mentally and physically. With love, I attempted to get him to open up so I could better understand the root of his insecurities and unhappiness. I learned almost nothing.

"What's going on, son?" I asked.

"Nothing, I'm fine," he said.

"Do you want to talk about what happened?"

"Not really."

"Did anything ever happen to you that I don't know about that you want to share? I swear, I will keep it between us."

"Dad, nothing happened!"

"I love you, son, I just want to understand so I can be in a better place to help you."

"I'm good."

Meanwhile, Mary and I continued to disagree on nearly everything, sniping at each other verbally and with disdain. The issue continued to divide us and hung like a dark cloud over every aspect of our lives. As my youngest son Barry pointed out, "Don't you see? The only time you guys fight it's all about Tommy."

We still went to sleep every night in dread, waiting for the phone call we were sure would come. When either of us came home from work, Tommy's presence on the couch or cooking pasta in the kitchen with his latest girlfriend would sour our moods almost immediately. With our eldest son studying overseas and his car sitting idle, we stupidly began allowing Tommy to drive again, likely a subconscious move to find some relief from his constant presence.

Things soon began to spiral downward, as his by-now-familiar descent into Oxy addiction resumed. His teeth began to turn a nasty greyish color as his personal hygiene deteriorated. We noticed him scratching his scalp or his arms a lot, sure signs of pill abuse. His sweet disposition again disappeared, replaced by snarly, terse replies to our questions or the vacant, dispassionate stares we loathed.

Tommy pulled into the driveway one night with the passenger window of the car shattered, pieces of glass all over the seat. His girlfriend's brother had punched it out in a rage during a fight with his sister, supposedly. Within days, Tommy got in an accident, and we yanked his driving privileges permanently but not before contending with the threat of a lawsuit and another spike in our insurance rates.

For a short time Tommy began seeing a new therapist, a streetwise, no-nonsense young woman who completely saw through his lying and BS. It seemed to be going well and there was another brief calm before the storm. Mary had been taking him, and the therapist wanted both of us to come with Tommy to one session. We were fairly certain he'd gone back to using pills based on his demeanor and hygiene, but he'd been insistent that he was only smoking pot. After a brief time alone with Tommy, the therapist summoned us to join them.

"Tommy's been telling me he's doing better, and that while he's not completely clean, he has stopped using Oxys," she said. "What are your thoughts?"

Mary and I looked at each other skeptically, and then glanced at Tommy. He stared at us intently to see what we'd say. After a long pause, Mary started.

"I don't know, I'm not sure I buy it," she said. "What do you think, Rick?"

"I don't know either; we've already been burned so many times that I can't tell the truth from lying anymore."

"Go ahead and drug test me," Tommy said, shaking his head in disgust. "You guys never believe me. I don't know why I even try."

"Why don't we believe you?" I asked in the slim hope we might find meaningful discussion that could lead to a breakthrough.

"Because of the past. You don't trust me."

"How do you get trust?" I asked. "Trust is earned, not given."

"By staying clean. Go ahead and test me so we don't have to keep having this annoying conversation."

"Tommy," the therapist said, "your parents are just trying to understand what's going on. Tell them what you told me."

"This is a huge waste of time," he said. "If you're not going to trust me, then test me."

We called his bluff. Mary left and bought a comprehensive screening kit from a nearby Walgreens and returned to the office. I supervised his filling of the urine cup to ensure he couldn't cheat, and then while he met with the therapist in private, waited for the results. Not surprisingly, the panel testing for the Oxy family of pills, long his drug of choice, tested positive, as did THC for marijuana. Confronted with the results, he now claimed that he'd taken pills just once a few days earlier, but wasn't taking them regularly. More lies.

As I drove Tommy home in silence, I felt my disgust and anger building. I'd worked very hard to try to open the lines of communication between us and make him feel accepted back into our family. His betrayal and constant lying made me realize I'd been suckered once again.

When we got home there was a FedEx package leaning against the front door. It was his Christmas present, an expensive ticket to a multiday concert festival taking place two weeks later that he would no longer be allowed to attend. He recognized it immediately, grabbed the package, and opened it.

It had long been determined that any money received from selling that ticket would become reimbursement for the hundreds of dollars in items he'd stolen from us. When I reminded him of this, Tommy convinced me to let him take the ticket because he had a friend who was going to buy it from him. Again fooled by his masterful manipulation, I complied. In the spirit of my new approach, despite the lies just experienced at his doctor's visit, I sought to give him opportunities to regain trust and reluctantly agreed to let him go sell the ticket himself. I made him promise to get me the cash and even said he could keep twenty dollars for food and spending money.

"You're a fool," Mary said derisively when I told her I'd given him the ticket. "We'll never see that money."

Not only was she correct, we also didn't see Tommy again for nearly three days. Cash in hand, Tommy did what addicts do. He went on a binge and spent all of it on drugs.

Once again our lives were engulfed in madness. Incensed that I'd been deceived and that once again he had stolen from us, I reverted back to the futility of trying to play detective. As I quietly worked my way through a dark lakeside park on a windy night looking for him, it hit me how ridiculous my actions were. But I was so upset and angry it felt better than doing nothing. Finding no clues in the park, I returned to my car and drove throughout the area, scouring familiar haunts and coming up empty. It was a fruitless effort to find a needle in a haystack. By now Mary and I weren't speaking to one another. Dejected, I headed to a sports bar to grab a bite and a couple of pints before heading home to the silence of her glares. She wasn't the only one disgusted with me. I'd become disgusted with myself.

The following day while at work, I received a frantic call from Mary just before lunchtime. On a hunch she'd gone to a garage apartment where a friend of Tommy's lived, and sure enough he was there, along with a 6'7" massive friend who had recently been released from jail. A screaming session ensued and ended with Tommy telling his mother how much he hated her and slamming the door in her face.

I completely snapped for the first time in months and left my office to race toward the house where Mary had found the pair. By now they were long gone of course, but that didn't prevent me from pounding on the door and shouting for them like a madman, baseball bat at my side in case the young giant decided to try to stop me.

Driving up and down nearby streets, I checked the 7-Eleven, the park they liked to hang out in, and other areas for what seemed like an eternity. Then in the distance I spotted a very tall man walking next to a very slight man, and recognized the color of Tommy's bright yellow soccer shirt. What a pair they made, a Mutt and Jeff linked only by a love of the drugs they shared and not any type of meaningful friendship. When I jumped out of my car near them the hollowness of their relationship was quickly revealed, as his "friend" immediately crossed the street and started briskly walking away as if he didn't even know Tommy.

"Where's my money?" I demanded, baseball bat still at my side for the misguided reasoning that the larger friend might be a threat. In reality, I was the one more likely to get arrested by wielding a bat in a quiet neighborhood at midday.

"I don't have it, it's gone," Tommy shouted. "Leave me alone, go away."

I walked back to my car and drove away, not expecting to see Tommy for a very long time, if ever again. My rage turned to tears and I sobbed uncontrollably as I tried to refocus on going back to work. *How many times by now have I found myself in this horrible state of grief?* I wondered at the time. *How much more can we possibly take?*

One night a few days after the street confrontation, Mary and I were in the kitchen when we were startled by a knock on our kitchen window. It was Tommy.

"Can I come in?" he asked. "I want to talk to you."

Apprehensively we let him in. Among the recently discovered missing belongings were my chainsaw and an expensive Bose speaker designed to play iPods, clear signs that Tommy had fully relapsed, as if we needed more proof.

"I've got a problem, and I need help," he said. "I've got to get out of Orlando."

As it had many times previously, false hope washed over both of us, and we immediately sprung into crisis mode. We began searching the internet and working phones with people we'd met through the support group to find the right program. *This time*, we thought, *we'll find the perfect program to help get Tommy sober.*

6

OUT OF SIGHT, OUT OF MIND

Sitting in a circle of folding chairs in the center of the room, we listened as stranger after stranger recounted familiar tales of pain, anger, and despair. From California to Maine, blue-collar towns to wealthy suburbs, the story was the same—drug-abusing children nearly destroying families and marriages.

The campus where Tommy now lived was more like a barracks than we'd imagined, a two-story brick building with the equivalent of an exercise yard on one side. Although no razor wire–topped fence surrounded the place, it quickly became clear that residents didn't see very much of the Utah sky or the mountains in the distance. From Tommy's room the focal point was a nearby Taco Bell sign, reminding him of food he couldn't taste and freedoms that he'd lost.

Tommy's residential treatment center in southern Utah, one of many throughout the United States, cost us more than

$6,000 per month. Diving tens of thousands of dollars further into debt was not something we wanted to do, but we felt it was our only choice. We often used the unfair analogy that if we had a kid with cancer, we'd spend everything we had to save him. We were hardly alone in our thinking.

Thousands of parents like us, from all types of different backgrounds and situations, plunge into enormous debt or pour their life savings into recovery programs that rarely yield successful outcomes. It is a thriving industry that preys on desperation and guilt.

This is not to suggest that there aren't some excellent programs and dedicated doctors, therapists, and counselors working in the recovery field; there certainly are. In some cases, such as my younger brother's, years of sobriety were achieved after just a few weeks in such a center. But to consider this route the only solution to a relatively unsolvable problem is like saying the only way to avoid an auto accident is to attend driving school.

Over the course of nine years that to date have involved at least thirteen relapses, detoxifications, and recovery attempts, we've concluded that many treatment programs are simply money pits. For some families, it's a way to kick the can down the road by paying enormous sums to try to solve their family member's problem. For others, it is similar to the purpose reform schools once served, allowing parents to maintain their busy lifestyles without the burden or embarrassment of a troubled child in residence. In the end, recovery and residential treatment centers, like any other business, exist to make money.

A 2015 documentary, *The Business of Recovery*, questions the effectiveness of expensive residential and outpatient programs,[1] an estimated $35 billion industry and growing.[2] Today there are more than 14,500 specialized drug treatment facilities in the United States.[3] Most are unregulated with marginal success rates, if any success rates are even tracked.

Our family made significant contributions to this business, incurring far more than six figures in debt tied to trying to save Tommy as he shuffled between various voluntary and involuntary treatment facilities during his late teens and early twenties. There seemed to be three common denominators. First, regardless of how dire the situation or how sick the potential patient, no one may enter through the gates until the facility is absolutely certain it will get paid. Second, anyone who enters will immediately meet brothers and sisters sharing an affinity for the same substances that landed them there, often creating alliances to depart and begin using again. Lastly, rarely do they work, resulting in massive amounts of money spent for an extended vacation from a problem that resumes once the money runs out, and often sooner.

Some may argue that we are just bitter over having spent so much money on a son who doesn't or won't ever get it. Others may conclude that we never found the right program. In our experience, recovery programs were mostly overpriced places focused first and foremost on raking in as much money as possible from desperate families and their insurance providers. These programs are the first to preach about how only an individual committed to change has a chance to get clean, yet they will gladly admit anyone forced to be there by court or family, provided they can pay. It's big business, plain and simple.

With substance abusers cycling through them like foraging ants in and out of their hill, it is virtually impossible to find meaningful statistics regarding success rates from treatment centers or twelve-step programs. Yet that doesn't stop "experts" from throwing numbers around.

The Sober Truth: Debunking the Bad Science Behind 12-Step Programs and the Rehab Industry, written by a psychiatrist who has spent over two decades studying and treating addiction, pegs the success rate of AA-based twelve-step programs at 5–10 percent.[4] A seasoned counselor and Narcotics Anonymous (NA) veteran I once discussed the subject with agreed with this assessment but pegged the recovery rate for opioid addicts, defined by him as staying off drugs for at least one year, at less than 5 percent.

Chasing real recovery success stats is akin to playing the carnival game Whac-A-Mole, minus a stuffed animal prize—the target is always moving and the misses are many. For starters, only about 11 percent of the estimated 23.5 million people age twelve or over with a drug or alcohol problem ever seek treatment, according to Substance Abuse and Mental Health Services Administration research.[5]

Meanwhile, those who do achieve success through treatment programs are rarely ever contacted again for follow-up, a friend who is a recovering addict recently reminded me. "It's been seventeen years since I completed my first rehab program, and not once has anyone from there contacted me since," he said, noting that neither his phone number nor address has changed.

Although real stats are as elusive as the problem itself, most people agree that opioid addiction is one of the very toughest dependencies to break.

For Tommy, landing in a Utah facility with other teen drug abusers was certainly not his choice.

"I hate this place," he told me. "They're only in it for the money, they don't really care. It's like being in jail."

Tommy's path since being hospitalized after we'd managed to find him in the decrepit naval barracks was very typical, we later learned. His first of thirteen detox and rehab attempts ended in less than a week, with his need to use drugs far greater than his will to stop. His initial rehab facility was located in the Florida Panhandle, and we decided that I would drive him up directly upon his release from the only hospital in our area with a mental health unit that included a drug detoxification program. There would be no chance to go home, no chance to run, no opportunity for either him or us to change our minds about what was to happen next.

Cruising up the interstate on the eight-hour drive, my son sound asleep in the seat beside me, it seemed like weeks had passed since the exhausting search and rescue of Tommy from the old building in Baldwin Park. It had actually been less than a week earlier. Since then we had scrambled to search any and all options available, both parents working the internet and phones. We knew that his hospital stay would be brief and were determined to send him straight into a rehabilitation program. Guilt again washed over me as I glanced at my son, still feeling then that I had failed him.

Along the way we stopped for food and he wanted to buy a book, *Into the Wild*, about a college graduate who had sold all his belongings, cut off contact with his family, and drifted throughout the United States before making his way to Alaska, where he perished.

"I want to travel, to see the world," he said. "I've never even made it to the West Coast yet."

"I get it, but first you have to get clean and get on track. You have a great life ahead of you, but the drugs will rob it from you if you let them."

The sense of relief I felt after checking him into the rehab facility was tremendous, though coupled with sadness. Looking back, I felt this same relief each time I'd drop Tommy at another detox or recovery center. Having somewhere to send him if even for only a few weeks allowed us time to regroup, recharge, and at least try to focus on our other children. Unfortunately, it wasn't very long before the vicious cycle would start all over again. It took years before we recognized what a waste of time and money most of this had been. It didn't solve Tommy's problem; it only briefly kept it out of sight and mind.

Driving home after dropping Tommy in the Panhandle, I meandered through back roads to give myself time to process all that had happened. We figured we'd have at least twenty-five to thirty days to plan the next move in regard to Tommy's recovery. We ended up having less than a week.

Within days of arriving, Tommy managed to get himself kicked out of the program by sneaking out of the center to buy cigarettes from a nearby Walmart for himself and fellow patients. Despite the lax supervision that allowed this and the fact that the center still had yet to assign him a counselor, his decision ensured that his stay was brief. Just a few days after dropping him off, I found myself back in the car for another sixteen-hour round trip to retrieve him.

Despondent again, Mary and I spoke on the phone repeatedly on my solo drive north. Back into crisis mode, we were running out of options and time. She furiously searched online and made phone calls, but finances, insurance rules, and the fact Tommy had now been asked to leave a rehab center left us with dwindling choices.

I'd begun that day at work, still relieved that Tommy was safely embedded in a program. The call came late morning that the center wanted us to pick him up by the following morning at the latest. While having dinner at a bar after my long drive back to the Panhandle that night, my phone rang. It was my brother.

"Send him to me, we'll take him," Ron said.

"No, we could never do that to you. Thank you, but that's not fair," I replied.

"I talked it over with Delores, and we can do it," he insisted. "He'll have to live by our rules, but he needs a fresh start somewhere where he doesn't know anyone."

Despite my protests, my brother remained firm in his commitment to help. Deep down I knew it was also the best option we had by far, both from a financial and practical standpoint. A family member, particularly one who had walked in Tommy's shoes and beaten the odds, would be far more vested in my son's recovery than a stranger possibly could, I reasoned. So began the first of my son's two multiweek tours in the mountains of northwest New Jersey.

7

THE TRANSPORTER

Like a scene from a spy movie, I quietly picked the "transporter" up at the airport late one night.

A burly, muscular man wearing jeans, a black leather jacket, and carrying nothing except a duffel bag, extended his hand after throwing his bag in the backseat.

"How are you? I'm Sal," he said in a thick Boston accent.

"I'm Rick."

"Look, I know this is hard, but I do this all the time, and it's gonna work out fine."

He had read my mind in the first fifteen seconds and put me at ease. He was a divorced former cop with a heart for helping troubled kids get on the right track. For a mere $3,000 fee plus expenses, he would fly anywhere, nearly anytime, to ensure the package—in this case Tommy—would arrive at the destination on time without drama.

After I'd briefly learned about his background, Sal asked me a series of questions and then began to go over the next morning's game plan. We would arrive to pick up Tommy from the hospital at 6:30 a.m. Sal would make it clear to Tommy that anywhere they walked, from the hospital to the car, the car to the airport terminal, even onto the plane itself, Sal would have his hand firmly on the back of Tommy's belt. Tommy was to walk slowly and deliberately in front of him, follow his instructions, and never try to deviate from this procedure.

Despite having gone through two recovery programs following two detoxifications, as well as a relatively successful twelve-week period of sobriety living with his uncle and cousins in New Jersey, Tommy had reverted to his destructive tendencies. The stealing to support his habit and his chaotic behavior had again become untenable in our home. Since a year remained before the legal pardon his eighteenth birthday would grant, we decided to force him into a residential treatment center in southern Utah.

Recognizing that my aging legs would have little chance of catching him should he decide to run, we hired Sal to help with the transition. Sal had successfully transported Tommy's best friend to a different state in the middle of the night without incident just a week earlier.

The next morning I picked up Sal from his motel and we drove to the hospital. While Sal met with him privately to explain the rules of engagement, I signed reams of paperwork to have Tommy released. We were soon in my truck, me as the chauffeur, Sal and Tommy in the backseat. Not much was said on the drive to the airport, and occasionally I'd glance in my rearview mirror and catch Tommy either staring vacantly out of the window or dispassionately at me.

At curbside, I said good-bye, tears welling up in my eyes, and hugged my son. "I love you, son. We want you to have a great life. Get clean! We know you can do it."

"Thanks, Dad, I love you too."

With that I watched them walk away, a muscular New England cop behind an emaciated average-height teen. As I drove away I questioned the decision to spend more money that we didn't have versus taking him out there myself. Many months later my son confirmed that we'd made the right call because, while waiting in the hospital, he had already thought through which stoplights on the route to the airport might be closest to one of his drug dealers' places and where the best spot to escape from my truck would be.

Except for one of the fathers in the circle who said nothing, my wife, Mary, was the last person to open up and share. I actually enjoyed it when the counselors rejected her pat comments and pushed her to dig beneath the surface of her emotions, which is still the level where she seems most comfortable. We were disappointed that we were barely allowed to see our son during this visit to a remote corner of the Southwest. By the end of the first day, we were reminded about a concept we had struggled to grasp in our Nar-Anon group back home. Family support groups are not about fixing the addict; they're about fixing yourself by learning to let go. We were also reminded that there isn't a thing any of us can do to rescue or help an addict; they must choose to help themselves.

Despite the intellectual fortification that Nar-Anon and family sessions at Tommy's various recovery facilities provided during the first couple years of our miserable voyage, they weren't enough to prevent futile and desperate rescue attempts or irrational behavior during emotional moments. Regardless of the advice and written principles urging us to "let go and let God," we simply were incapable of doing so. In a now familiar combination of despair and anger, I'd regularly jump in the truck on a night he had quietly disappeared in a futile attempt to find him. I would drive up and down row after row of cars through apartment complexes or shopping centers searching for the blue Prius with a particular bumper sticker driven by Tommy's best friend. I'd stroll through dangerous streets and dark city parks at night with the illogical thought that I might come across him. Doing something felt better than doing nothing.

There were times when my irrational approach led to confrontations, accusations, and potential harm. I could feel the desperate rage boil up inside me and know it was wrong to put myself in danger, but I was unable to back down. Like the superhuman strength from adrenaline that supposedly allows a person to lift a car off someone under it, when my emotions rose on the battlefield in the fight to save Tommy, adrenaline took over and I sometimes lost control.

The most poignant moment of our first visit with Tommy in Utah came when he told me, his tears flowing, "I'll never have the chance to walk across that stage and get my diploma. I'll never enjoy that moment of graduating from high school like a normal kid."

His words, especially the word "normal," pierced my soul as the truth of his words sank in. He saw himself as an outcast, barely worth our efforts.

Like previous attempts at recovery, and attempts yet to come, the months in Utah ended in failure, not to mention more debt. Again we found ourselves struggling to cope with a seemingly impossible dilemma. My brother stepped forward a second time with great courage and selflessness. With nowhere else to turn, we looked north once again.

The energy-sapping gray skies of a New York winter were a familiar sight as my son and I sped in the rental car around the mountains toward my brother's house in northwest New Jersey.

"It really looks different up here in the winter," Tommy said. "With the leaves off the trees you can see everything."

"Wait until you experience a couple arctic cold blasts, then you'll really know what winter is about."

Upon arrival we all sat around Ron's living room for an intervention of sorts, an establishment of ground rules that, not surprisingly, Tommy was ultimately unable to abide by. My mother, Isabel, then eighty-five, Delores, and my two young nephews and niece were present as my brother laid down the ground rules. My youngest nephew, Jake, curled up on Tommy's chest, the recently formed bond between them one of the only positive outcomes of the ongoing saga. My mother tossed out a typically annoying comment in her best schoolteacher tone. Delores made sure he knew that he'd be doing his own laundry and reminded him of rules for keeping the house tidy. The kids weighed in enthusiastically that they wanted Tommy to stay. Tommy promised to abide by all rules, which he did until around the time of his eighteenth birthday, when all the parental strings on him were officially untethered. Thus began his second stint in New Jersey.

By the time I returned a few short months later, the wheels had fallen off. A few days prior to Tommy's birthday, Ron and Delores left for a much-deserved vacation in the islands and to get married in a private ceremony. It was just the opening

Tommy was looking for, and on the first weekend with my elderly mother in charge, he decided to go "camping" with some friends and didn't show up back home until 4:00 a.m. Once Ron found out, it ended quickly. He called Tommy to kick him out and called me to tell me what happened. The next day I boarded a plane to New York.

The following weeks would bring Tommy to death's doorstep and put him into yet another codependent relationship. But first he manipulated and conned us into thinking everything was still on the right track. From about age sixteen, he had regularly expressed his intense desire to be on his own, not to have to answer to his parents or, for that matter, anyone else. On his birthday, Ron and Delores still away, I picked him up at a diner and with my mother in tow headed to Manhattan for a birthday dinner. A good friend, whom my children call Uncle Bob, joined us for a pleasant and uneventful evening at a family-style Italian restaurant.

Bob has a special place in all of our children's hearts, as he does in both Mary's and mine. My best friend since college, he accompanied all three of my sons and me on our wilderness trips and is like another father to them. Bob, who tragically lost his only son, Bobby, at a young age to a rare flu virus, enjoys spending time with all three of the boys and Jessie, and they all love him. It was Bob who cheered Tommy up during a five-day rafting trip down the Colorado when he felt bad about not being a strong enough rower or was picked on. During the difficult years of Tommy's struggles, Bob was a constant source of strength and encouragement to me on the darkest days.

The next morning would foreshadow the days to come. Tommy wanted me to drive him to a friend's house before

I went into the city, which I gladly complied with. On the way we stopped to look at his friend's beat-up car, which of course Tommy had no money to buy but thought I might cave in and spring for. His halfhearted efforts to find a job had yielded no opportunities, not surprising given the region's high unemployment and depressed economy.

He was squirrely as I tried to drive him to a destination that he didn't quite know how to get to. Finally he directed me into a neighborhood, where he wanted me to drop him at a park in the middle of several houses.

"Why don't I take you to your friend's house?" I asked.

"This is fine, you can leave me here," he replied.

"This is BS," I responded, feeling the tension and fear well up inside of me.

"He doesn't want his parents knowing someone is coming over," he lied.

"So they won't see you walking up?" I demanded.

"They're at work," he lied again, deploying the circular logic that we'd sadly come to recognize.

As he got out of the car, I could feel hot tears of rage building up. I drove from the neighborhood, turned around, and circled back on another street to see him from a distance. He was standing at the edge of the park on the phone. He spotted me and started walking toward the car. Finally forced into telling at least a partial truth, he admitted that it was a couple high school girls that were coming to pick him up and that there actually was no friend in that particular subdivision, just a convenient meeting place.

"I love you, Tommy, get clean!" I implored, driving away and gasping for air under the all-too-familiar waves of pain and despair. My wife's "I told you so" response when I shared the episode on my drive to the airport turned my hurt into anger and, once again, Tommy's problem drove a wedge between us.

That morning was the last time I saw Tommy for several weeks, and very nearly the last time I saw him alive.

8

BOOMERANG OF AGONY

With excitement and surprise since he hadn't mentioned any-thing, I saw my son Barry jog out with the offense for the spring varsity football game. The defensive captain, he had not played a down of regular offense since his sophomore year. But now he was lining up at both fullback and tight end.

Just then my cell phone rang. It was Tommy, whom I hadn't heard from in weeks. After leaving another treatment program in Delray Beach before completion, he had worked his way back up to Orlando and was sleeping on the couches of friends. I got up from the bleachers and walked down to the sidelines where I could still keep an eye on the game while talking. As soon as I got to field level, Barry caught a short pass in the backfield, turned the corner, and ran for a fifty-three-yard touchdown, the only one of his varsity career.

How ironic and typical, I thought. A potential highlight memory virtually erased by the timing of a phone call. My joy quickly turned to dread. Instead of enjoying this moment with my wife and friends in the stands, I was sucked right back into the life-draining cesspool of addiction. When I reflected on this a few hours later, I felt that God was reminding me not to get too high or too low about anything in life. The message seemed to be to keep things in balance and remember that he, not me, was in control.

As for the urgent phone call, Tommy wanted me to buy him a pizza to be delivered to the friend's place where he was staying. No hello, no update on him returning to Orlando, just another self-centered request. "No," I responded and hung up.

But just as he'd done countless times before, he managed to divide his parents again. Before I could get back to my seat in the stands to tell Mary that he had resurfaced, Tommy had already called her, and she had paid for the pizza to be delivered.

The statistics regarding opiate addiction are frightening and getting worse. According to the CDC, more than ninety people per day are still dying from opioid overdose (including prescription opioids and heroin) in the United States alone. This "epidemic," as the agency labeled it, has surpassed car accidents as the leading cause of accidental death in our nation and has claimed over five hundred thousand American lives since 2000.[1]

Tommy was on the brink of joining these statistics at least twice.

During our first year of misery, we never fathomed that we'd still be living in the destructive wake of a synthetic heroin user years later. Or that the numbing cycle of drug abuse, lying, stealing, detox, rehab, and relapse would repeat itself thirteen times. After digesting many books and occasionally attending family support groups, we began to recognize how powerful chemical dependency truly is. As our understanding about addiction grew, so did the tension between Mary and me about what to do.

Each journey to another recovery attempt was somewhat surreal and was always a trip I took alone with Tommy. It was almost the same each time, making me feel like the Bill Murray character in the movie *Groundhog Day*. Each trip would begin with relief that he was still alive and a small glimmer of hope. As I would watch my broken son snooze next to me, whether in the passenger seat of the truck or on an airplane, I could never understand how this peaceful, artistically gifted, and love-filled young man had fallen so low. Each time I found my mind and heart overwhelmed with memories from happier times.

Tommy had the magic touch when it came to fishing. If we had four lines in the water, his pole was almost always the one bent over with a fish on the line. He often rode off on his bicycle with rod in hand to fish for bass in the small lakes near our home, either alone or with a friend. His gift for painting and other artistic pursuits became obvious when he was very young, and his colorful landscapes and ceramics can still be found throughout our home. A gentle boy, Tommy loved all land and sea animals, dolphins being his absolute favorite. He couldn't stand to kill even an insect, preferring to scoot one onto a newspaper to transport it safely outside.

At the beginning of each desperate, yet futile, attempt to help Tommy keep his demons at bay, he was pensive and calm, as if relieved to still be alive. It was as though each journey served as a much-needed vacation from the drugs that so firmly had him in their grip. But it was never long before old patterns returned; a nastier or indifferent temperament was the first sign that he was again using.

During Tommy's first stay in northwest New Jersey, Uncle Ron made a tremendous and generous sacrifice to demonstrate what a clean and sober lifestyle looked like. For ninety straight days, he took Tommy to a Narcotics Anonymous or Alcoholics Anonymous meeting, quite a feat given the remote location of Ron's home near ski resorts in the Ramapo Mountains. After most meetings they would go out to eat, bowl, or play miniature golf with other recovering addicts of all ages, illustrating that it was possible to have fun without adding drugs or alcohol to the mix.

"How's he doing?" I asked during one of the many phone conversations with my brother.

"He's doing pretty well, but I'm still not sure he's committed," Ron said. "He's really immature for his age and continues to hold on to the notion that pot is not a drug."

"What about at home; how is he getting along with Mom, Delores, and the kids?"

"Oh, the kids love him, and Mom is Mom. It's all about her. At the same time, she's really happy to get to know another of her grandkids. She's getting old so we give her a lot of leeway. After all, when you've lived alone as long as she has, it's hard not to become focused on yourself."

For a few months Tommy did well under Ron's tutelage, even sometimes working days in Ron's automotive business. Lazy by nature, Tommy even had the "pleasure" of changing tires on an auction lot during the frigid Jersey winter. During the occasions it was not smooth sailing, Ron found it very difficult to distinguish between what was normal seventeen-year-old angst versus the manipulative behaviors associated with addiction. Toward the end of Tommy's first Jersey adventure, I got a sobering call from my brother.

"Look, I hate to tell you this, but I think he's slipping. Also, his drug of choice is the worst one to overcome and has the lowest success rate of any others."

We knew by then that Tommy had been using pills, having identified some found hidden in his room, and we knew from drug tests and hospitalizations that opiates were in the mix. What we didn't understand at the time was the difference between dependency on opiates and other substances, such as the cocaine that had nearly destroyed my brother many years earlier.

"Help me understand, what does this mean?" I asked.

"Basically there are depressants like alcohol; uppers such as cocaine, meth, or speed; and hallucinogenics like LSD or mushrooms. Tommy has the very worst type of addiction and hardest to kick, essentially pill-form heroin."

"So what does heroin or Oxys do, what's the high all about?" I asked.

"That's the problem, it's not about getting high," he said, his voice becoming more somber. "It's about escaping reality entirely. It's about not feeling any pain. Over all the years I've been in the rooms [where AA and NA meetings take place], very few opiate addicts are ever able to kick it." He paused. "Sorry, bro."

Tommy had a knack for finding the person least serious about sobriety at any meeting or rehab center he attended, a point Ron noticed immediately. Usually this was a woman who was as fragile as he was. His typical pattern was hooking up with a woman in recovery, developing a codependent relationship with her, then both of them returning to the drugs. As my brother warned him countless times, the worst thing you can do for yourself while trying to get clean is get wrapped up in a relationship. "Fix yourself first," he would say. "Only then are you capable of having a meaningful relationship with someone else." Ron, who met his first wife in recovery, spoke from experience.

As with every other piece of advice Tommy received during this phase in his life, the warning fell on deaf ears. During his second stint in New Jersey, he met a woman ten years older than him at a meeting. They soon stopped attending meetings, and she introduced him to the deadly cousin of Oxys—street heroin. Days later he took a lethal dose.

9

CHEATING DEATH

Less than twenty-four hours from the decision to jump on an airplane in our most dramatic (and as usual, fruitless) rescue attempt thus far, my stress levels were through the roof when Paul finally wheeled into the airport. With no time to spare, we threw some of his belongings in my truck, parked, and rushed to get through security.

Safely on our way to New York, Paul asked, "What's the plan, Dad?"

Sadly, I had none. "I'm not sure, son, what do you think?"

A week earlier came the news that we'd dreaded but were not shocked by. Tommy had begun using heroin. A particularly lethal batch of heroin had already caused numerous deaths in New Jersey. As whiskey is to liquor, heroin is to drugs, the substance with not only the worst reputation but also a track record to support it. Heroin is a killer that creates a dependency that is exceptionally difficult to overcome. Despite the fact that the Oxys and other pills Tommy and his friends had been snorting or smoking were just as addictive and potentially deadly, essentially lab-made heroin, there was something about hearing your kid had shot up the real thing that hit us hard and sent my mind racing.

Maybe sending him to New Jersey a second time was not such a good idea, I thought, as my brother's words fully sunk in. Did we simply kick the can down the road yet again, taking advantage of the only option we had to get him out of our house again without adding to our huge pile of debt? Were we still looking for a silver bullet like we had by shipping him off to Utah? What if sending him back north only added to his feelings of rejection and worthlessness? In retrospect, each futile attempt to try to fix Tommy was spawned as much by selfish desperation to table the madness at least for a few weeks as it was to try to cure him. At the same time, there seemed few other choices beyond pushing him back onto the street. Mary and I were at each other's throats, our other children were suffering, and our home environment had deteriorated into constant tension and strife. Having both grown up in chaotic and dysfunctional households, Mary and I may have been too quick to pull the trigger on sending Tommy off to the next program in our desperation to restore calm. But none of this mattered when I heard what my brother said next.

"Rick, there's more," Ron said. "He overdosed and had to be brought back."

Tommy had no prior experience with heroin until this point, at least to our knowledge. Typically, he stubbornly refused to heed the warnings of others, shot up a large amount, and overdosed on his first use. Looking back, it is conceivable that he simply had enough by this point and tried to end his pain. Regardless, he passed out, his heart stopped, and for a few seconds was technically dead. Only through the grace of God was he not alone. Friends performed CPR and were able to revive him very quickly without him losing much oxygen to his brain. It was more than forty-eight hours before any medical supervision entered the picture. The day after his first overdose, three recovering friends from the support circle Ron had introduced Tommy to showed up at the home of the twenty-eight-year-old woman Tommy had been staying with. In a brave intervention, they forced him into their car and then into a rehabilitation center. Four days later, now eighteen, Tommy checked himself out and reclaimed his phone along with his other belongings. His first call was to the girlfriend, where he returned to live. Despite having cheated death, he still didn't believe he had a serious problem.

10

RISE OF THE OPIOID KIDS

In the late '70s, Colombian cartels established cocaine distribution networks in the United States, beginning in Miami, and by the early '80s cocaine had spread throughout the nation to become a mainstream recreational drug. Shortly after, crack cocaine, which was usually smoked instead of snorted, emerged as a cheaper alternative. Crack, often cut with other toxic substances to increase drug dealer profits, decimated many depressed inner cities and rural areas and continues to do so. During the early '90s, the methamphetamine plague spread from largely rural northwest home garage labs to the rest of the continental United States. The crystal meth problem, depicted by such TV shows as *Breaking Bad*, exploded once home chemists figured out how to create their own supplies using such toxic substances as battery acid, drain cleaner, camp stove fuel, and camera battery lithium. Even worse than the original lab version created in the '70s for West Coast biker gangs, the new homemade meth was even more addictive and featured such long-term, nasty side effects as open sores, rotting teeth, and permanent brain damage.

Like these earlier drug epidemics, the opioid problem now claiming thousands of American lives each year continues to be driven by greed. A far cry from the meth cooked up by a fictional Walter White in a beat-up RV, Purdue Pharma created OxyContin in a state-of-the-art corporate laboratory, launching the FDA-approved product in 1996. As with other twentieth-century prescription drugs that were initially deemed safe but proved harmful, it took more than a decade for officials to acknowledge there was a problem. When looking back over the past century at how poor a job our federal agencies and elected officials have done protecting its citizens from dangerous prescription drugs, it becomes obvious that, as in many other parts of our broken government, big lobby money has trumped public good. Uncanny parallels exist in the time cycle—from FDA approval to product launch, market adoption, user addiction, and finally regulatory action—tied to various "revolutionary" painkillers launched over the decades.

Consider oxycodone, the first semi-synthetic opioid, which was invented by two German scientists in 1916—not coincidentally after the United States banned heroin—as a pain relief substitute for heroin, morphine, and opium. Just as Purdue did eighty years later with OxyContin, oxycodone's creators touted the substance as nonaddictive, claims that later were proven false. Products containing oxycodone were not approved in the United States until 1939, and today several remain on the market. In 1950, a new prescription pain relief drug combining oxycodone with aspirin, Percodan, emerged. Similar to what transpired with OxyContin, it took more than a decade before regulators addressed a Percodan addiction problem. About thirteen years after Percodan's introduction, California's attorney general blamed it for one-third of all drug addiction in the union's largest state, but it took another seven years for the DEA to get around to listing oxycodone as a Schedule II controlled substance with high potential for abuse. The mid-sixties Rolling Stones' song "Mother's Little Helper" was a nod to the largely hidden but growing prescription drug problem, aired nearly fifty years before our current opioid epidemic took hold. Despite the fact that opioid overdose is claiming significantly more lives each day than did our country's bloodiest military conflicts, it remained in the shadows until 2016, dismissed as an affliction mostly limited to inner-city neighborhoods or individuals on the fringe of society.

This begs the question, how many lives and families might have been saved over the past century if lawmakers and regulatory officials had done more to listen to scientific and medical warnings about the potential dangers of new drugs flooding the market thanks to the fast-growing pharmaceutical industry? Confusing, complicated warnings listed on pill bottles or read by announcers at breakneck speed on TV commercials are not enough when it comes to substances that can create dependency after short-term use. Some of these products should never have reached the market in the first place. But the Big Pharma lobby machine made sure they did and has also made sure that efforts to restrict access to pain pills have been slowed.

Since 2003, Big Pharma has spent $2 billion on federal lobbying, more than any other industry except the insurance industry. Even more disturbing are the enormous sums Purdue and other drugmakers keep spending to protect their "golden goose" pain pills long after the growing opioid epidemic became well documented. From 2006 through 2015, Purdue and the makers of Vicodin and Fentanyl spent a collective $880 million on campaign contributions and lobbying efforts to influence legislation, according to the Associated Press and Center for Public Integrity.[1] These expenditures were about two hundred times more than what advocates seeking to restrict access to medical narcotics such as Oxy-Contin spent during the same time frame and eight times more than the powerful gun lobby spent. With an army of more than thirteen hundred lobbyists canvassing all fifty state capitols and Washington, DC, its Pain Care Forum doling out deceptive information, and with seventy-one hundred political candidates receiving opioid lobby contributions, it becomes clear why politicians and government officials have kept their heads buried in the sand for so long. Flush with Big Pharma cash, most lawmakers simply keep looking the other way or, worse, are complicit by voting against measures intended to curb abuse.

Efforts to change this pathetic situation continue to be countered by profit-protecting pharmaceutical companies. While they publicly espouse support for efforts to curtail opioid abuse, behind the scenes pharmaceutical lobbyists continue to fight back in every way possible.

In the same year President Obama trumpeted his administration's $1.1 billion initiative to tackle the opioid epidemic, maximizing publicity through a Prescription Opioid and Heroin Awareness Week, he quietly signed into law legislation greatly reducing DEA-enforcement powers.

Authored and sponsored by elected officials beholden to the drug industry lobby, the Ensuring Patient Access and Effective Drug Enforcement Act of 2016 effectively loosened restrictions put in place earlier, requiring the DEA to warn and work with law-bending drug wholesalers and distributors such as pain clinics before prosecuting them. Behind a public smokescreen that spotlighted legitimate patients such as seniors who were having a tougher time getting their prescription opioids under the new, tighter system, Big Pharma won again, rolling back some of the strides to restrict access.

Easy access to the drugs opened a doorway that led to full-blown addiction for Tommy and countless other central Floridians when pill mills began popping up like mushrooms on a rain-forest floor flooded with direct sunlight for the first time. As is well documented, Oxy pills were easy to find whether you were looking for them or not. At one point around this time, long before I knew the first thing about the drug, our family doctor had prescribed a bottle for relief from some excruciating back pain I'd been experiencing. The following day with my back hurting during my drive to Miami, I realized that I'd forgotten the entire bottle on a high shelf in our kitchen. Calling Mary, I asked her to put them in a safe spot. It was too late; the bottle was gone. Since this was before we'd discovered Tommy was using, and likely before he'd even found his way to the drug, we were perplexed. Mary suspected the painter, who just happened to have begun a job at our house that day. Insulted and somewhat perturbed at being accused, he insisted that neither he nor his crew had anything to do with the missing bottle of Oxys. But nearly a week later the phone rang and he apologized. He and his wife had discovered that his twenty-something son had an Oxy problem and later found my now-empty pill bottle in their trash.

In 2010 the DEA led a major sweep across our region to shut down many pill mills being run by unscrupulous doctors, and the following year Florida lawmakers passed two laws mandating electronic prescription-tracking systems and various other measures designed to restrict pain pill access. We were pleased at the time, believing that would aid our efforts to keep Tommy away from opiates. The crackdown initially worked, with Oxy use dropping for the first time in years. But like trying to plug a hole in a dike under pressure from a wall of storm water, a new leak sprung up in its place in the form of street heroin. With family medicine cabinets now empty and pharmacies under scrutiny, substance-dependent users could no longer afford or find the pills they'd become hooked on. They turned to the only option left, the street, with deadly results.

Drug dealers gladly picked up the slack, and the problem worsened. Unlike the lab-made products they'd relied on, at least understanding something about dosages and effects, the black market opioid pills and heroin were often cut with dangerous chemicals such as Fentanyl, said to be up to one hundred times stronger than morphine. Intended for doctors to deliver via hospital IV or patch to patients recovering from surgery or battling severe, painful conditions, Fentanyl dramatically amped up the impact of any opioid it was mixed with. It was and is cut into heroin or street versions of oxycodone or Percocet to stretch drug dealer supplies and profits. Almost immediately, the Orlando region and other areas saw a frightening spike in overdose deaths.

Tommy first found his way to heroin in New Jersey but discovered the black market pill forms upon his return to Florida. The feelings of boredom, restlessness, and invincibility that led to reckless and stupid behavior during my own teen years remained alive and well in my son. Only this time it was not alcohol or marijuana being used by restless youngsters. Self-medicating kids seeking an escape now had tiny, nearly impossible to detect pills at their fingertips—agents of death that parents such as Mary and I initially had no clue about. Lacking odor or obvious symptoms, opioid use was relatively easy to hide from parents, school officials, and other authority figures. There was no smell of booze or weed on their breath or clothes. There were no telltale signs of bloodshot or glassy eyes. The opioid kids typically showed few if any signs that anything was wrong—that is, until it was nearly too late.

Despite the fact that shortsighted lawmakers and regulators didn't foresee the inadvertent consequences of clamping down on Oxy access, their first steps to require prescription monitoring and put pill mills out of business worked. Walgreens, CVS, and other reputable retailers did their part by moving some meds behind the counter and requiring proper ID for filling a single prescription of opioid-based drugs. The DEA continued to keep the pressure on pain clinic doctors and owners, which had been scooping up vacant strip center bays as fast as fly-by-night mortgage brokers—that is, until 2016 when the "patient access" act passed by Congress and approved by Obama largely neutered the agency.[2] With DEA prosecution efforts undermined by the Big Pharma–engineered law, it was back to business as usual. Many of the same bad actors arrested during the pill-mill crackdown have since rebounded, indicates a recent Johns Hopkins study, which reports that a relatively small group is again accounting for a disproportionately large share of the opioid prescriptions being written.[3]

Sadly, Big Pharma's stranglehold on lawmakers continues unabated, and along with it any meaningful change attempts. Awareness certainly rose after President Obama, moviemaker Rob Reiner, state governors, senators, and many others finally dragged this long-neglected issue into the light beginning in 2016. However, the millions being spent by opioid profiteers to influence policy in their favor continue to ensure that aggressive doctors can overprescribe, that shady pain clinics and distributors receive ample warning before their licenses are stripped, and most of all, that the profitable pipeline feeding an epidemic of their own creation keeps flowing. Drug companies and their investors will continue to happily feast while their products find new users and inflict financial and psychological tolls on families and on those lucky enough to survive.

11

THE ABDUCTION

I tossed everything I'd learned thus far about managing emotions and not being able to control an addict out the window as I raced toward the airport in my latest fit of stubborn desperation. My heart was racing, and all I could think about was not getting to New Jersey in time. Paul added to my stress by nearly missing our flight, booked late the previous night; he showed up with minutes to spare. Once on the airplane we caught our breath. Both of us saw this as a final desperate attempt to save Tommy's life. We would stop at nothing to bring him back to Florida, even if it meant physically kidnapping him. Our thinking was unrealistic and foolish.

"So what's the plan, Dad?" Paul asked once we were airborne, a very reasonable question.

"I have no idea," I answered. "What do you think?"

Having sprung back into crisis mode the prior evening when the call came that Tommy had checked himself out of rehab and was back with the older woman he'd been living with, I'd barely had enough time to rearrange my work schedule, book one-way flights, and throw a few things in a duffel bag before racing to the airport. Figuring out how we might convince or force Tommy to come back with us hadn't yet entered my thoughts. Tattered and torn from the ongoing Tommy saga, I was extremely grateful to have Paul with me and not be going alone.

As Paul and I devised what seemed like a reasonable plan, it occurred to me how much I now viewed him as a fellow adult and not just my oldest son. His impulsive and out-of-control behavior had given us fits during his challenging middle and high school years. The clean-cut, handsome guy sitting next to me still sometimes did stupid, impulsive things, but had matured into a smart and focused young man. He knew where he was going in life and was determined to get there.

"How about this?" he said. "I spoke with Tommy this morning and told him I was coming up to visit him. He didn't sound great on the phone, but seemed genuinely excited to see me."

"But he has no idea I'm coming?"

"No. We need to figure out how to keep you out of sight so he doesn't run."

Tommy said he and his girlfriend would pick Paul up. Paul suggested that when we arrived at the airport, I would lag behind. Once they'd driven off, I'd pick up a rental car and drive toward my brother's town for a later rendezvous once Paul managed to get Tommy alone. Ron had warned us that Tommy seemed to be under the strong influence of the girlfriend, which was nothing new when it came to Tommy and females.

Less than five minutes after turning our phones back on after touchdown, we had to scrap our plan. Tommy and his

girlfriend had driven to the wrong airport! Instead of New-
burgh, New York, they were at Newark, New Jersey, likely
two hours away given traffic. Scrambling, we identified what
looked like a reasonable meeting spot on a map, and Paul told
Tommy he'd take a cab there. Speeding down the highway
to drop Paul at a diner before Tommy got there, I began
to realize what an ill-conceived game we were playing. My
love and desperation had buried any rational thought. But
it was too late to turn back. Nearly an hour later I watched
from a hidden vantage point as Paul got into the car with
his brother and the girl outside a New Jersey diner. Minutes
later I learned that plan number two would also have to be
scrapped.

Texting me from the backseat of the girlfriend's car, Paul
informed me that they were heading into Manhattan for dinner. I implored him to get back to the girl's house as soon
as reasonably possible but knew I was in for another long
and wasted night. Following a two-hour stint working on
my laptop at a Borders with Wi-Fi, I sought a place to wait
it out. At least there was a Yankees game on television at the
comfortable bar I found, but the wait for them to return from
the city seemed endless. Finally, a little after 10:00 p.m., Paul
texted me to let me know they were driving back. Tapping
my phone's navigation app, I plotted a route to wait near
the woman's apartment building, where it turned out she
was living not just with Tommy but also with her mother.

As I drove into the dark corner of the convenience store
parking lot near the apartment, I again felt foolish for thinking this had any chance of working. Perhaps I'd watched
one too many action films or TV dramas. As if in some
Hollywood-made stakeout, I patiently waited. Paul texted

that he had convinced Tommy to take a walk, the first time he was away from the girl in the seven hours they'd been together. After what seemed like an eternity, I saw the familiar shapes of my two eldest sons ambling up the dark, quiet street. It wouldn't be quiet for long.

As shocked as I was by Tommy's rough appearance, a new tattoo joining the earrings he now wore in both ears, he was far more stunned to see me. His reaction was rage.

"You set me up!" he yelled at Paul. "What the hell is he doing here?"

The tension on both sides immediately skyrocketed, as I said, "We're here to take you home."

After a brief and heated exchange of words, Tommy sprinted into the shadows with me in futile pursuit on a bad ankle. I shouted for Paul to cut him off, but it was no use. He vanished.

Anger turned to rage before rage turned to despair.

"What the hell are you looking at?" I screamed at a couple onlookers who were staring at me in the parking lot as I walked back to my car, feeling the tears well up in my eyes and dread ball up in my heart. "Mind your own business!"

Paul showed me where Tommy had been staying. There was absolutely no way I was leaving now. My emotions more controlled, but not by much, I banged on the door of the apartment and could easily have soon found myself under arrest. The girl's mother began shrieking at Paul and me to get off her stoop.

"Get the hell out of here or I'll call the cops!"

"Go ahead, call them. It will be fun watching you explain to them how your twenty-eight-year-old daughter committed statutory rape with a minor under your supervision," I said, forgetting in the heat of the moment that Tommy had just turned eighteen. "How about a local TV station showing up with their cameras; would you like that?"

I'd managed to direct all my anger about my son's situation at this woman whose only crime was having enough pity on a lost, otherwise homeless teenager to let him sleep on her couch. Blame based in wrong righteousness is the worst kind.

Thankfully the woman's boyfriend stepped outside and immediately diffused things.

"Go inside, honey," he said, taking a big drag from his cigarette. "He's just worried about his son. I've got this."

When Paul and I shared our story, he listened intently. He then shared with us how deadly the batch of drugs was that had briefly killed Tommy a few days before. As later confirmed through internet searches and my brother's network, several kids in the area had already died from the "black tar," the man told me. After he and I spoke a little more, everyone was calm for the moment. Paul was able to get Tommy to answer his call and convinced him to speak with us in a parking lot about a block away that was surrounded by woods on two sides and would afford Tommy easy escape paths if necessary.

Like a tense hostage negotiation, Paul led the discussion. Still determined to bring him back home, I wasn't particularly open-minded to alternatives.

Tommy seemed dumbfounded that we were even there, still feeling angry and betrayed by Paul's actions.

Paul and I pleaded with him to return with us, and he refused. All three men shed many tears as we discussed his situation and relentlessly tried to change his mind. Around and around in circles we went for about an hour, Paul and I pulling every lever we could think of and Tommy, his mind clearly fogged by drugs, coming up with one illogical excuse after another for staying in New Jersey. Exhausted and under extreme pressure, Tommy finally agreed he would come home a week later once he'd had a chance to say goodbye to his friends in New Jersey.

The next morning Paul and I drove to the airport in relative silence, dejected by what we both perceived as complete mission failure. The next day I purchased a one-way ticket from Newark to Orlando for six days later. Neither of us expected Tommy to get on that flight, and it wasn't until I saw him walk down the airport hallway in Orlando that I actually believed he did.

12

PILL MILLS, POLICE, AND PAIN

Sages of the recovery industry warn that the definition of insanity is doing the same thing over and over and expecting different results. It took us years to understand this. It's our son, we rationalized repeatedly—and periodically still do today—and we love and can save him.

It didn't take long for our household to descend back into a state of dysfunction when our son once again became ensconced in our lives after his return from New Jersey. At first there was a sense of relief; at least he was alive and back with a family who dearly loves him. The hugs were many as we began a futile attempt to return to family life as normal with Tommy back in our home. As was his habit, Tommy soon latched on to another girlfriend, one he met through attending the Narcotics Anonymous meetings we required as a condition of his living with us.

For a few weeks he did a good job complying with our curfews and rules, all part of the agreed-upon contract that he'd signed to live with us again. But his efforts to find a job were pathetic and unproductive. Like a vampire, he wanted to sleep late, lie around all day watching television, and then come alive to go out at night. We berated him about getting a job, since he had promised this, and he'd give the same lame answer every time: "I submitted applications online." There was a complete lack of motivation tied to his underlying problem.

It didn't take long for Mary and me to begin snapping at each other again and disagreeing about what to do next. Meanwhile, sketchy characters began showing up at our home, creating an embarrassment for our youngest son and potential threat for our young daughter. Barry, imposing at six feet tall with a lean, muscular build, began confronting such kids with regularity. He'd walk toward them in a menacing way and shout at them to leave our property, sometimes when they were just a few steps down our driveway.

"He's not here, this is his parents' home, get the hell out of here!" I heard him yell one day to a completely stoned-out kid with long hair who was beginning to amble toward the front walk. By now Tommy's siblings had had enough.

"He's an idiot," Barry said. "Why do you keep letting him come back here? He just eats your food and steals our stuff."

One night our dog started barking crazily. Tommy's girlfriend stepped outside to talk to an unknown visitor. As I got up to see what was going on, Tommy went racing past me to the door, baseball bat at his side. Thankfully my youngest and eldest sons were not home, and my daughter was asleep in her room. I stepped into the madness to intervene when

I saw Tommy's girlfriend getting into the face of the young man, whom I recognized as an old friend of my son's, now fully grown.

"Get in the house," I ordered the girlfriend, in no mood to have another mouthy agitator in the mix. Disgusted with the chaos that my addict son had brought to our front doorstep, I snatched the bat from Tommy's hands and got between him and his ex-friend.

"Tommy owes me money," he said.

"Get out of here," Tommy shouted.

The anger in Tommy's face frightened me. Only once before had I seen my mellow son exhibit such rage—in the convenience store parking lot when I'd surprised him in New Jersey. I sensed he had returned to using.

After calming both of them down, I asked the boy to leave my property with no resolution in what was clearly a drug debt dispute. It wasn't the first time someone had come searching for money they were owed due to our son's addiction, and it certainly wasn't the last. But it was the final straw.

The next day we asked our son to leave, and he gladly complied. After sleeping on various friends' couches or park benches, he eventually squatted in an empty home of a friend and fellow drug abuser whose parents had recently moved away and put their house on the market. Breaking into the now-empty house he had been raised in, Tommy's friend invited him and another drug-addled teenager who had also been sleeping outside on benches to join him. For several nights the delusional trio had the place they'd dreamed about, where no parents could interfere with their desires to use the drugs they craved and sleep as late as they wished. However it wasn't long before neighbors caught on to the situation and alerted police. Tommy's friend who had grown up there was arrested for assaulting one of the officers that evicted them and was thrown in jail.

Our son the master manipulator soon contacted us to apologize and pledge his commitment to staying clean. We reluctantly let Tommy return and for a few weeks things went fairly well. With my assistance, Tommy got a job working at a local restaurant. But just a few days later the restaurant's general manager, whom I knew, warned me that he was pretty sure Tommy was using pills. He'd seen it before and saw the same symptoms in our son. Less than two weeks after starting the job, Tommy was fired for not showing up or bothering to call. It would be the last job he worked at for nearly two years.

Despite Tommy's obvious inability to function in any normal capacity, Mary remained insistent that attending college as a full-time student was the change he needed. I reluctantly agreed that it was worth a shot, even though I knew down deep that the chance he'd be able to handle this was remote. Tommy, of course, had other ideas. His desire remained to "get a job, get an apartment, and go to community college." Completely out of touch with reality, he clung to the notion of independence without the first clue of what type of consistent commitment and amount of money this would require.

Mary was insistent, and she wore both of us down. I finally went along, both to keep what little peace remained between my wife and me and to get him out of our house. The final decision was made following an emotional, irrational discussion.

"You're going to college, that's it!" Mary shouted at him. "You took a spot from someone else, and you're going to honor that commitment!"

Reluctantly Tommy agreed, and once again we resumed the charade of normalcy and proceeded to make plans to get him off to college. Mary went into her mommy mode of shopping, leaving no detail unaccounted for in getting him ready to move into his dorm at a college 150 miles away. Less than a week before he was to leave, the phone rang at about 2:00 a.m. Tommy and his best friend had been arrested for painting graffiti on a local parking garage. Their immature excuse demonstrated the stupidity in their judgment. In their hazy minds they had decided to do something to commemorate their friendship on the eve of them going their separate ways to pursue higher education. Again we rescued him, with the punishment consisting of the two young teenagers painting the garage wall they had defaced and the owner luckily not pressing charges.

Hope takes many shapes when you find yourself in despair, and it became hard to distinguish between reality and illusion. In looking back upon the lengths we went to get Tommy to complete high school online, get accepted to a decent college, and actually move onto that campus, it's hard to fathom how much denial we were actually in about our son's condition. As my brother puts it, "Denial is more than just a river in Egypt." A person who cannot function at a high enough level to hold an entry-level job is certainly not ready to successfully manage a full course load amid the distractions of the college experience.

Tommy lasted about one month. It was clear from our early phone conversations that things weren't going well. We'd asked him to email us progress reports and none came. We learned he'd already been disciplined for cursing at a resident assistant. I drove up to visit him on a Sunday, planning to go kayaking or spend the day at the beach. When he got in the car, I could sense it was already over.

"Son, you're not going to classes, are you?"

"No," he said, his voice cracking and the tears beginning to flow. "I can't do this, I'm just not ready."

After a quick lunch, I drove him back to the dorm and began the two-hour drive home. The next day we withdrew him, and I drove back up to gather my son and his belongings. For the fourth time that year, Tommy returned home.

He again signed a new behavioral contract spelling out the conditions that would allow him to live under our roof. Within a few days he began ignoring these rules.

Near our home we found a teen support group run by a no-nonsense New Yorker, a recovering addict herself. Very few if any of the teens attending were there by choice, with some there by court order and others as minors forced into the group by their parents. During our first family group session, Mary and I were reminded yet again how widespread the problem of teen drug abuse really is.

By now the media was beginning to shine a light on the pill-mill industry, but very little was being done to address it. In the absence of prescription monitoring technology, blocked in Florida by the drug lobby despite its successful introduction in several other states, Oxy enthusiasts were able to fill a single doctor's script from a pain clinic as many times as they'd like by visiting multiple chain or independent drug stores in an area.

With years of easy access thanks to pill mills and no monitoring, trafficking networks had been established from Florida into many other states. Dealers brought Florida Oxys north up I-75 into Georgia, Tennessee, Kentucky, and West Virginia, where it became known as "hillbilly heroin." It traveled across I-10 through the Panhandle into Alabama, Mississippi, Arkansas, and other points west. It flowed up I-95 into the Carolinas and northward.

Though we had no idea at the time, we found ourselves at the epicenter of the escalating opioid epidemic during the exact same time period that our highly sensitive and unsure teenager was coming of age.

Initially, we felt a small sense of relief when attending support group meetings. There was some measure of comfort in finding we were not alone in the agony of dealing with an addicted child. But as our son's many rehabs and relapses continued, such meetings became a source of frustration.

"How come our son is the one that never seems to get it?" Mary asked on the ride home from a meeting.

"I don't know. Maybe it's his lack of spiritual acceptance; it seems to be an important step. But I know what you mean. After all we've been through it gets hard to listen about how great everyone else's kid is doing."

Later when we understood that most "successes" were very short-lived, we softened on this stance and sought to help others instead of feeling sorry for ourselves. We witnessed an all-too-familiar pattern of pain, heartache, and despair at each gathering of anxious parents and spouses. While the situations and stories differed, the essence was the same—drugs arresting the emotional development of children, or adults, and turning them into expert manipulators, liars, and thieves.

Supplementing the costly outpatient program Tommy now attended were regular NA or AA meetings we would drive him to on weekends and during the week. He soon developed an interest in a girl who would accompany her mother to some of the groups, a destructive pattern that would repeat itself again and again. Ron had previously warned us about Tommy's tendency to gravitate toward the people in a group who were least serious about getting clean; it was as if he could immediately sniff them out. The fact that Tommy had yet to find a sponsor since returning to Florida was another signal that he was going through the motions and appeasing us by pretending to be serious about recovery. Like several other members of his teen group, Tommy was telling counselors what they wanted to hear, beating the drug tests with his medicine-dropper-filled-with-Clorox trick, then secretly using again on the sly.

For my brother, clean and sober for more than twenty years and a veteran of trying to help teen users, the clearest sign that Tommy was faking it came at a Narcotics Anonymous convention session where a recovering addict shared his story. While many audience members were tearing up at the devastatingly familiar tale, Tommy sat emotionless, stone-faced, my brother reported.

The descent from obvious pot smoking back into pill abuse was rapid. We soon found ourselves in the hellish and familiar pattern of waiting for the phone to ring in the middle of the night when he didn't come home. Other nights of exasperation I'd stupidly burn more gas by driving all over the city searching for him.

The return of his defiance brought things to a head, and it was clear something had to change. On the early Sunday evening before his second stint in a hospital detox unit, I sensed he was about to leave for good. In retrospect, we probably should have just let him walk out. Instead, we pushed the panic button when I found his backpack full of clothes on the grass under his bedroom window behind our house. Mary called the police while I tried to keep him from leaving. The situation turned chaotic when he tried to run. Again desperate to save this person I loved deeply but no longer knew, I put my arms around him and restrained him, refusing to let him leave. Going berserk, he began screaming how much he hated us, and we fell to the living room floor. It became an ugly, shameful scene with my daughter crying, wife screaming, and youngest son entering the fray. My son pulled me off Tommy and convinced Tommy to speak quietly with him in his room until the cops arrived.

Playing the good cop, bad cop approach perfectly, the two officers who responded convinced Tommy that getting help was his best option.

"Do you want to be arrested? Look at how much privilege you have here. I'm thinking you need a good long stay in jail to wake you up," the one policeman said sternly. "Your parents don't deserve this; you need to get a grip."

While the policeman walked into another room to speak with Mary, the "good cop" began talking to Tommy. I could still hear my daughter sobbing down the hall.

"What are you using?" he asked.

"Just pot," Tommy lied, his eyes nervously darting across the room at me.

"Look, I know this is hard and you're going through a tough time," the cop said. "Since we've been here I've seen you scratching yourself, and I'm pretty sure you're using pills. Just be honest with me. Are you using pills?"

Both policemen had noted the constant head scratching, darting eyes, and general irritability associated with opioid abuse.

"Yeah," Tommy said quietly, his eyes now looking at the floor.

"Which pills?"

"Mainly Oxys."

"Look, you have good parents, a great home, and a family that loves you. Will you let them get you help?"

"Okay. I need help."

Within minutes we were in the car and heading for the emergency room of the same hospital we'd taken him to many months ago after coaxing him out of the abandoned building following his first disappearance. I knew that he was only here because he'd been forced into it and had no choice. As I sat in the emergency room again, waiting several hours for the process of evaluation and admittance to play out, a hurricane of emotions wracked my soul. Disbelief that here we were again, heartache for the low self-esteem that must have led my son to pills, anger over my stupidity for not seeing the signs, sadness over his lost childhood. I prayed for answers, yet began to question my faith, much like a survivor of a loved one who has been taken at far too young an age. What purpose could God have in mind for continuing to test us and ravage our family in this way? There was also, as became typical after future relapses, a sense of relief that he was getting help and would soon be out of our home. At least for a few days there might be some peace.

Driving through the empty 4:00 a.m. streets on the way home, I convinced myself that this would be the time that Tommy would get it and move forward with a productive and happy life. This sliver of hope would always appear during the first five years of our family ordeal. I could not fathom then how much worse the situation would eventually become.

13

PLANNING
THE FUNERAL

It took eight days from the time I dropped Tommy off in South Florida the first time until the "experts" deemed him completely detoxed and ready for the next step in his recovery. He was transferred to an allied recovery center and was thrown out after two weeks for not following rules and arguing with counselors. After a long weekend sleeping on benches and scrounging for food, he showed back up at the recovery center on Monday, and they gave him a second chance.

Was this rehab attempt number six or seven? I wondered at the time. Tommy had been homeless and living on the streets at least twice before that we were aware of, and he certainly knew how miserable an existence that was. But to an addict, the craving for drugs is far more powerful than all other considerations.

At first Tommy seemed to be making the most of his second chance, and over the next three or four weeks we received glowing reports from his counselors on how he had turned the corner and was working the twelve-step program. He had even landed a job working in a local coffee shop where owners embraced his quirky style of dress. We were delighted to hear this, yet our enthusiasm was tempered by past disappointments. We made plans to visit him with his siblings on the following weekend since it was our only chance to get together as a family that Christmas season.

When we arrived in Delray, we went to pick him up at the coffee shop. He was behind the cash register wearing bright green plastic sunglasses without the lenses, a baseball cap on backward, and a colorful shirt that matched the hippy vibe of the place. Most encouraging was the fact that he was smiling, something we had not seen from him in a long time, and bantering with customers in a friendly manner. He seemed happy.

Less than twenty-four hours after the most optimistic, enthusiastic conversation we'd ever had with one of Tommy's counselors, the phone rang and the bottom dropped out again. The same counselor, speaking in a low tone as though he was about to inform us our son had died, told us that Tommy had been kicked out of the center for good and was on the streets. They'd found drug paraphernalia in his duffel bag, and the word on the street was that he had shacked up with a girl he met in the program and was using hard drugs again.

His quick spiral back into self-worthlessness and abandonment of recovery apparently began after an accident that wasn't his fault. While skateboarding back to the recovery center from his job, he was hit by a car that ran a stop sign. He was thrown over the hood and broke his arm. Worried this would prevent him from being able to work at the coffee shop and that he'd lose his job, he immediately became depressed and within days had turned back to drugs for solace.

Fragile. It's the word that best sums up Tommy's condition during the years of his struggle and the only word that explains why he would so quickly plunge back into the abyss after any setback. So low was his opinion of himself that he would immediately throw in the towel rather than fight through a challenge or moment of adversity. Every one of his thirteen relapses was triggered by either a painful event or his eventual lack of stamina in a challenging job. Neither his parents, counselors, siblings, nor doctors ever really understood the depth of the pain, insecurity, and hypersensitivity to others and the world in general that shaped Tommy as a person. He was always somewhat fragile. The escape through drugs made him even easier to break.

This time it was the skateboard accident that caused him to give up.

By the time the all-too-familiar call came in from the recovery center, we were already relatively numb, despite having let slight hope shine in just a day earlier at the coffee shop. The most important thing we've learned over the past eight years, something that parental love makes nearly impossible to abide by, is the concept of never getting too high or too low on the inevitable roller-coaster ride of having a child who is an addict. As disheartening as it was, when we hung up the phone our reaction was different than it had ever been before.

"That's it, we're done," Mary said.

"It's over," I agreed.

For the first time we were united in our decision and firm in our resolve. We were not going to lift a finger to help him, and in no way would we allow him to again destroy our family or home. We had other children to care for and our own health to be concerned about.

Mary had been through two cancer surgeries and another major surgery during the time that the struggles with Tommy had been going on. I'd been through an ankle surgery and found that my blood pressure had been climbing to dangerous levels. I'd also gained a lot of weight and was drowning my pain by drinking too much. The stress related to our son's disease had taken its toll on all of us, and we could not allow this to continue.

About a week later Tommy called and we both got on the phone.

"I'm homeless, I've got nowhere to go," he pleaded, sounding like he was crying. "Please send me money for a bus ticket home."

"Whose fault is that?" we responded. "No."

"I'm probably going to die then," he whined, pulling out all the tricks that had manipulated our emotions and decisions in the past. "So you don't care?"

"We love you, Tommy, but will not help you unless you commit to being sober," we said, hanging tough.

"I hope you find me dead," he said, hanging up the phone.

What a great way to kick off the weekend, receiving a phone call from your homeless addict son saying that he'll soon be dead if you don't help him. But we were prepared and had reached the point of separation necessary both for him to have a chance and for us to keep our sanity.

Reflecting on those several weeks, from when he relapsed prior to leaving for South Florida through him resurfacing in Orlando, we essentially mourned the loss of our son. It was as if he was already dead. When thoughts of him would enter my head, on an airplane, while driving, sitting at my desk, I'd be swept with grief and sadness, frequently crying, my heart constantly aching. I would pray for God to awaken his spirit, to save him from the drugs that had abducted his life, but I struggled to truly believe that my prayers would be answered. I sought for reassurance, but down deep had lost faith and therefore found none. Our love for Tommy never wavered, but to cope we had to mourn him and move forward. Mary later confessed to me that she'd lie awake in the middle of the night and plan his funeral arrangements in her head. We both had lost hope.

Over time, we realized we had reached what the professionals call *detachment*. Largely through the efforts of a great therapist who has become my friend, I learned to acknowledge my emotions when thoughts of Tommy entered my mind. Instead of simply burying them in shallow graves where they'd eventually surface in fits of anger or self-destructive behavior, I learned to acknowledge them and then shove them aside.

We learned through the insidious grapevine known as Facebook that Tommy had returned to Orlando and was staying with various friends. He claimed to only be drinking and smoking pot. He didn't try to come home and would not have been allowed inside had he tried.

One night I was about to drive past a McDonald's a few miles from our house when I saw a familiar silhouette slinking toward the side door. I wheeled into the parking lot and saw my son shuffling toward the bathroom inside. In the car two spots down were two completely wasted-looking male teenagers and one female. After a few minutes Tommy walked out of the restaurant like a zombie, eyes completely glassed over, hat on sideways, earrings dangling, and wearing a black-and-white checkered jacket accessorized with lime green sneakers. He had clearly used the bathroom to shoot up.

"Hey, Tommy," I called through my open window. In a daze, he shuffled over to the side of my car and muttered, "Hi, Dad. Hey, I've got to go."

"Come with me," I pleaded, desperately wanting to take him for coffee or at least have a few minutes to connect.

"Sorry, Dad, gotta go."

The others all eyed me suspiciously as Tommy climbed back into the beat-up car, and they drove off. It was clear he was back on the hard stuff, the path that leads only to prison or death. We had resolved not to allow him near our home, but we did cave in and order him a few pizzas during the time he spent with friends. But that too soon came to an end when his lying, stealing ways caught up with him. Before long he was homeless again and living on the streets.

14

FLEAS, FIENDS, AND FRACTURES

The shift in the tone of Mary's voice in the kitchen told me something was terribly wrong. We were about to shuttle some of our friends to the airport after the surprise birthday bash weekend that my wife had staged for me, including a great party featuring my friend's band.

"What! Oh my God!" she shrieked, the blood draining out of her face.

Well, at least his overdose didn't ruin our great weekend, I morbidly thought, immediately feeling guilty and selfish.

"Tommy's in the hospital and has been since Saturday," she said after hanging up the phone.

By now Tommy was sharing a flea-and-cockroach-infested trailer in an unincorporated rural slum east of Orlando with his relatively long-term girlfriend and an older man she called her uncle, but who wasn't. In the poor judgment typical of drug abusers, Tommy and his girlfriend had decided on a dark Saturday night to drive an old scooter, capable of top speeds in the thirty to thirty-five miles per hour range, on a major four-lane road into Orlando. He later claimed to have been trying to attend my surprise birthday party. Whether the back taillight of the scooter was working remains a mystery. What is known is that a large car traveling sixty to sixty-five miles per hour ran the scooter down from behind, launching both passengers, neither wearing a helmet, many yards through the air. Somehow both survived, landing in grassy areas rather than the pavement. They woke up in separate hospital rooms the next morning, neither remembering how they got there.

Self-esteem is a complex recipe stirred by experience, circumstance, brain chemistry, and many other factors. In my case the lack of acceptance from a detached father, coupled with a medical side effect that left my teeth somewhat gray and without enamel throughout my grade school years, made me insecure and desperate for acceptance by the time I reached my teen years. For my son, never finding his tribe and feeling like the odd man out in his own family led to feelings of worthlessness, social anxiety, and over time drug abuse.

Perhaps it is my own low opinion of myself as a kid that has made me so keenly empathize with the pain my son wrestles with. The daily school bus ride during my early years was a terrifying experience. Some of the single-cell teenage miscreants that rode my bus full of kids ranging from kindergarten to twelfth grade took great pleasure at picking on the younger kids, particularly anyone with an obvious physical weakness. "Black teeth" was the name they abused me with, sometimes several of them chanting this in unison. By the time I was nine or ten years old, my tears had turned to rage, and sometimes I'd try to fight back. These were futile attempts that only turned the verbal abuse physical, and more than once I got off the bus bruised and bloodied.

Even to this day there is nothing that infuriates me more than a bully picking on or taking advantage of others perceived as weak or defenseless, an internal anger that likely began with the nasty, ignorant teen schoolboys who once tormented me. My willingness to take on bullies—from a man using a crowded subway car as an excuse to inappropriately rub himself against a young woman to an abusive colleague taking advantage of a shy new worker—is a risky approach. It is probably wiser to ignore such issues, but my inability to do so, especially when someone is being bullied, has created a few problems over the years, including a couple brushes with serious injury or death. While I've certainly become more selective with age and in recognition of our increasingly dangerous world, there are still times when walking away from an injustice just doesn't cut it.

For Tommy, who is slightly built, it wasn't physical characteristics that crushed his self-esteem during his formative years. It was more his inability to achieve a sense of belonging. The tribe of outcasts, consumed with the culture of drugs, was the only place he found the acceptance he craved. He tried becoming part of many groups and succeeded for a while in some, such as the Boy Scouts and crew team, but he ultimately took up full-time residence on the Island of Misfit Toys.

At the hospital where Tommy and his girlfriend Sarah were recovering from their accident, we felt genuine pity for the young woman we'd grown to loathe but had never really had a full conversation with. Wrapped in a body cast and clearly in pain, she looked so sad, lost, and tiny, more like a twelve-year-old than the eighteen years she actually was. Suffering from a broken pelvis bone, shattered shoulder, cuts, bruises, and other unknown ailments, Sarah had suffered the worst from the scooter accident. Our son had some bruised ribs, lots of cuts, bruises, and road rash, but by comparison was unscathed. When we later saw pictures of what was left of the twisted wreckage of the scooter, we couldn't believe either had survived.

By now Tommy had not been living with us for several months. The previous summer had been a disaster, culminating with his arrest for selling narcotics just a couple months before the scooter mishap. We found out about the arrest through the internet mug shots that Mary obsessively and covertly viewed on a daily basis, making sure I was unaware of her activity.

At first we were relieved, feeling that perhaps a few months living in the harsh reality that is jail might wake him up, but mostly knowing it would be harder for him to die from an overdose on the inside. But within two days Tommy had been bailed out by his primary drug dealer, further increasing his debt to the 350-plus-pound giant whom we later recognized on the nightly news following his arrest during a major sting. The scooter accident didn't seem to even faze our son, and he was right back to resuming his synthetic heroin habit and living in one of the most dangerous neighborhoods in the city.

Within a couple of weeks, his drug debts must have become due, because Tommy, now nineteen, was forced by gunpoint into a room at his drug dealer's house, where he was kept locked in for a week and pistol-whipped at least twice. As previously mentioned, by now we had already accepted and mourned our beloved son's imminent death and had begun to move on.

Somewhat to our amazement, we got a call from Tommy asking for help just a few weeks after we saw him at the hospital.

"I really want to get clean this time," he pleaded after we greeted his request with skepticism.

Once again false hope rose up in our hearts. *Will we ever learn?* I thought as we drove to pick him up.

He was in really bad shape this time, with sores, bruises, filthy hair, and discolored teeth. Now weighing only about 125 pounds and wearing tattered clothes, he looked more like a person who'd just been released from a prisoner of war camp than someone we used to know. His mother was thrilled to have him home and alive, even if only for a day, and cleaned him up, tried to get him to eat, and was actually in a good mood for the first time in weeks.

As much as we love our children and try to be good fathers, there's simply no way a father can have the same bond with a child that a mother can. We didn't carry them inside our bodies for nine months before going through the difficult and miraculous process of bringing them into the world. As Mary hugged, cried, laughed, and doted over our broken son, I felt very little this time beyond the intense desire to get him back out of our house. Emotionally, I'd completed the mourning process. Having this person back in my home, someone who had hurt both my wife and my health, tanked our finances, and nearly destroyed our family, was nearly too much to take. Yet here we were again.

With very little hope that he'd really changed, we entered him into a detox facility the next day. From there he went into another rehab program, this one only ninety minutes away. For the first time ever, he actually completed the fifty-three-day program and received a graduation certificate at a ceremony we attended. It was during family meetings at this center that we were exposed to the scientific aspects of addiction, including how hard drugs can rewire the brain, but that a sober brain, much like a liver, can regenerate itself over time. We also learned how much drug abuse retards development, particularly during the teen years when the brain is going through its most active development phase. Our nineteen-year-old was developmentally about thirteen, the head counselor told us.

On the ride home, Mary and I were elated with the idea that through sobriety Tommy still had a chance to repair the damage he had done to himself. We'd previously believed his drug use must have caused irreparable brain damage and fretted that he'd never be able to live a normal life, even if he did manage to get clean. The new information was a glimmer of hope that we prayed our son would grasp. He didn't.

Upon graduation from the program, Tommy insisted on returning to the "love of his life," Sarah. We knew from texts, phone records, and social media that she was desperately clinging to their relationship. Sarah, whose young mother had died from an overdose the year before and whose father was not in the picture, was as codependent on Tommy as he was on her.

Determined to forge his own path, Tommy decided to move into a halfway house in Daytona Beach that was linked with the center he had graduated from. Like other halfway houses he has since resided in, it was an old, no-frills house in a relatively rough neighborhood. Run by a hard-nosed military veteran, it seemed just the place for Tommy to have a chance to thrive. He lasted about a month.

Never since his struggles with opioids began had Tommy managed to stay clean beyond ninety days. It was almost as if an internal timer went off that it was time to use again. He would do so well, even going to meetings every day and sometimes trying to work the twelve steps toward sobriety. But just as quickly he would crash, picking right up where he left off. Within days he'd find himself back at either the grim reaper's or jail warden's door.

Tommy and his girlfriend manipulated Mary's mom into taking both of them in to live with her once he'd had enough of the halfway house rules. It went downhill quickly, with the pair stealing and pawning his grandmother's silver and Tommy being arrested for shoplifting about a week later.

His grandmother bailed him out without our knowledge, and Tommy decided he wanted to try getting clean again. The only good news from the mess in our minds was that he still wasn't in our home or town and that the time periods between relapse and attempts at rehab seemed to be getting progressively shorter. With this rationalization, we again sanctioned a return stay at the rehab center he'd successfully attended before, putting as much of the exorbitant cost through our insurance plan as possible, but again increasing our astronomical debt load. Our love was too great to give up now.

At home, family dynamics continued to shift. The stress on our family was especially hard on my daughter, who finally had come to accept that her favorite brother was gone.

"*That* Tommy is gone forever," she told me one day, a sad look in her eyes. "I don't know this Tommy, he's different." By now our other sons were fed up and advising us to just let him go and stop trying to help him. We'd already been through several attempts at rehab and recovery, none of them successful for more than a few weeks.

But as I told Tommy repeatedly during my delusional phase of trying to reason with an active opioid user, "We'll never give up on you, son; don't give up on yourself."

While we refused to quit on him, we made it clear that this was his final chance to receive any assistance from us. Little did we know then how foolish this promise was or how often we would go back on the vow.

On one such occasion, after Tommy had resurfaced and called his mother, it was my daughter's softball game that was interrupted.

"I'm going to get him," she said.

"No you're not, I'll get him," I insisted.

Both of us put ourselves in harm's way several times when it came to this struggle. When I was out of town, Mary didn't hesitate to venture into dangerous neighborhoods in the middle of the night, a fearless, five-foot-tall, petite, and weaponless warrior that should never be underestimated. When it comes to one of her children, she's as fierce as a lioness trying to protect her cubs from a roaming male hoping to take over the pride.

As I drove toward the rendezvous spot, fighting my cynical frustration at our latest Groundhog Day morning, Mary was scrambling to find a detox facility with an open bed and a recovery center that could take him after that. As usual, it was the weekend, and the business staff was off duty. By now experts in the recovery business, we knew full well that no matter how bad a condition Tommy was in, there would be no room at the inn without the requisite financial payments up front. There was no time to spare.

"Can you wait until tomorrow to leave?" I asked Tommy after picking him up on a street corner. He was carrying his remaining clothes and belongings in a tattered garbage bag, the drawstring plastic ties over his shoulders like the straps on a backpack. He reeked of cigarette smoke and body odor as he slung the bag into my backseat and climbed up front.

"No, I really need to get out of here today," he said.

"Why, what's going on?"

The fear in Tommy's eyes seemed different this time. It was not the fear of dodging a drug dealer to whom he owed money, even though those threats still existed. It seemed to be a deeper, more genuine fear than I'd seen before.

"I've got to get out of Orlando," he said. He began to sob.

As much as we'd already been through, a small doubt had remained in the back of my mind that perhaps he wasn't truly an addict, as I then understood an addict to be. I'd grown to detest the label *addict*, much as I'd later learn to hate the word *disease*. Both seemed overly simplistic, convenient ways to put addiction into a neat little box. There is nothing remotely neat about addiction.

As I tried to comfort my crying son, putting my hands on his shoulder and reminding him how much I loved him, I realized why his fear was different this time. He was so firmly in the grip of the drugs he'd been using that he knew unless he was immediately extracted from his familiar stomping grounds, he'd likely die.

Mary called to say she'd found a highly regarded program in Delray Beach, which was known in the dysfunctional family circles we now traveled in as the recovery capital of the southeast. There were numerous rehab facilities located there, and we put the wheels in motion. First he would detox at a facility near the center to work through the physical withdrawal process, which was always painful and messy. On the car ride to the detox center, Tommy began experiencing cramping and nausea, the first stages of withdrawal. I explained to him that if he chose not to complete the program, he should not bother calling us again. At the time we meant it, but we really never could turn our backs on him. Each time a brief period of sobriety would grant us enough time to rejuvenate mentally and physically, and because the time between relapses and sobriety kept getting shorter, we kept clinging to the hope that this would be the time he'd really get it.

Tommy and I arrived at the bleak, white-brick detox building, located in a deteriorating neighborhood. The woman at the desk was gruff and no-nonsense, but her eyes harbored the kindness and understanding of a person who had seen scores of kids like our son. After a brief physical and interview process, she suggested I go and buy him some packs of cigarettes.

"Honey, the one pack he's got isn't going to cut it!" she said.

It was very odd to buy cigarettes for the first time in more than twenty years, especially for my child, but I complied. I gave Tommy a huge hug, told him I loved him, and urged him to work hard at his recovery.

"You can do this, son," I said.

"I love you, Dad," he said.

"I love you too, son."

After dropping the cigarettes back at the center, I began the three-hour drive home. Easing back onto the interstate I was swept by the familiar relief that he was no longer in our care, at least for a while, and for the first time in months I allowed myself a small measure of hope that he might get better. This turned out to be the last time for a few years that I had real optimism and hope that my son would have a happy future. Hope neutral is the gear I chose to remain in, and still mostly remain in today.

15

GROUNDHOG DAY
(THE MOVIE)

Four hellish years, nine rescues, nine detoxes, nine rehabs, and nine relapses from the time we found Tommy in the abandoned naval barracks, we found ourselves driving Tommy back to the halfway house in Daytona for a second tour of duty. While the mix of men living in the house seemed more compatible with our son this time, we honestly didn't expect the outcome to be much different. And it wasn't.

For several weeks Tommy worked at a seafood restaurant cutting fish, shucking oysters, and frying seafood. While the hours were decent, his unrealistic expectations about buying a car, getting his own apartment, and attending college right away clearly signaled that little had changed in his drug-addled brain. Perhaps even more disconcerting at the time, approaching double digits in relapses, was the fact that he clung to the notion of being able to smoke pot and not do other drugs.

Like clockwork, at about the ninety-days-sober mark Tommy gave up on what he called "Dirtona," and began snorting and shooting up Oxys again. He reunited with his girlfriend Sarah, who by then had found work as a stripper. The two of them flopped wherever they could, at friends' houses, drug dealer couches, the fleabag trailer where her raggedy, twelve-tooth "uncle" lived, or whatever park bench they found themselves near during their drug-fueled haze.

We didn't hear from him during this period, but we changed the code on our garage door keypad and the locks on our doors for fear of being robbed by him.

The accident, as much a fault of his poor judgment in taking a low-speed scooter onto a major highway as it was the driver that mowed Tommy and his girlfriend down, produced a substantial insurance settlement check for him. The dumb-luck, American-liability lottery at its finest! He used the settlement money to buy a used car and landed yet another restaurant job he'd soon abandon. We knew Tommy was alive mostly by the toll bureau invoices that continued to arrive in the mail, indicating his regular habit of running tolls.

Before long Tommy was flopping in the house of his morbidly obese drug dealer. Clueless, he had returned to the same place where he'd previously been abused and held at gunpoint! Not surprisingly, Tommy's drug habit must again have racked up substantial debts to this guy, because before long we received a call from the insurance company that his car had been involved in an accident. It turned out that the dealer had appropriated the car as collateral for Tommy's debt and was driving it when the accident occurred.

Mary, who sometimes seems to thrive on confrontation, was soon on the phone with the dealer himself, a nasty and loud conversation based on the end I could hear. The dealer threatened to have the car sent to a chop shop and dared my petite wife to come down there to get it. Bad idea. Mary was able to connect with Tommy and, by herself without my knowledge, drove down into the middle of the crime-ridden neighborhood to rescue our son yet again. The stolen car report she had filed worked, and within a couple days we got a call from the police that the car had been retrieved; we paid to tow the battered vehicle back.

After my wife retrieved Tommy without incident, I returned home from a business trip to find our emaciated son curled up under a blanket on our couch. I wrestled with a blend of pity and disgust. This time we decided to do his detox at home, determined not to spend another penny on anything insurance didn't cover. It was a nasty process with · the vomit bucket, sweats, chills, and mood swings associated with withdrawal and detoxification from pill-form heroin. He mostly just slept or whined. After a few days, Tommy was ready to give Delray Beach another try. Like a scene from *Groundhog Day*, I was again behind the wheel of my truck for a long ride, my relatively incoherent, barely functioning son riding shotgun.

Christmas season came quickly that year, and neither Mary nor I were much in the mood to deal with the shopping, hustle, and over-commercialized ruination of the season. We were exhausted, physically and emotionally. By now I'd ballooned to my nearly all-time high in weight, continuing a yo-yo with weight that had to put a huge strain on my heart and other vital organs. The signs were not lost on my doctor, who warned me to get healthier or not expect to live to see grandchildren. For Mary, it was the level of stress that concerned me most, given the scientific linkage between stress and cancer. Our daughter developed a very unhealthy addiction to food during this period that she continues to battle, and her size also continued to increase.

The deep frustration I'd harbored toward my son began to morph into resentment, as I recognized the physical ills and emotional scars he'd inflicted on our family. Much like when visiting my estranged father prior to forgiving him for being a lousy dad, I grew to dread having to visit Tommy and was relieved when I left. The day after Christmas we wrangled our other three kids into the car despite their protests and made the three-hour drive south to see him. After a relatively forced reunion and lunch, Tommy returned to his recovery center and we returned home.

In January Tommy moved into his third halfway house in eighteen months, this one in South Florida. The cycle continued. Each time the story was the same. Our slim hopes that he would finally "get it" would soon be dashed, and we now had reached eleven rehab attempts, not to mention the misery of eleven relapses, rescues, and detoxes. By now, one painful rescue attempt after another had blurred together, and today we're not certain how many times our son tried recovery and failed. One morning while I was finishing this book, my wife and I spent more than forty-five minutes on the phone trying to piece together a timeline of all centers, jails, halfway houses, and jobs my son had held during this four-year period, even going through file folders and bank records to try to jog our memories. Suffice it to say, we didn't keep a journal and never got to any definitive answers. We had spent these years, and the years prior and since, simply trying to survive the ordeal ourselves while keeping our son afloat.

By the end of 2013, Tommy was attending an outpatient program thirty minutes away, after somehow convincing us to break our vow never to have him live with us again. He had at least separated from his codependent girlfriend, Sarah. As usual, he did well for a while, but it didn't take long before familiar patterns began to emerge.

First, he found a new muse, a sweet girl a few years his elder who was also fighting to beat synthetic heroin. Unlike previous girlfriends our self-loathing son connected with, this young woman seemed to be good for him. At first it was purely platonic, but by the time she left the boyfriend she'd been living with and who had supported her recovery attempt, it became clear that she'd fallen in love with our son. This was a big mistake, especially for her. My clean and sober brother had long ago warned against dating addicts. He spoke from experience. He'd married and had two children with one before divorcing.

"Fix yourself," Ron always admonished. "Learn to love yourself before you even think of trying to have a relationship with someone else."

Tommy, of course, still wasn't ready to listen and didn't. Missy and her long-term boyfriend split up, and it became clear to us that she and Tommy had crossed the line from being just friends. It wasn't very long before his built-in sundial completed its circle, and he returned to the hard drugs again.

As much as I'd developed a fair amount of self-pity regarding our son's addiction and how harshly it had impacted our lives, it felt minor compared to the tragedy that had crushed my closest confidant and friend, Bob.

Bob and his then-wife, Shelley, brought a beautiful boy whom they named Robert into the world. Years earlier, prior to any children, Bob, Shelley, Mary, and I, along with our respective dogs, had lived together for a year in a one-hundred-year-old, three-story Colonial-style house Mary and I had purchased to restore. By the time Robert Jr., "Bobby," came into the picture, we had just welcomed Barry into our family. Bobby was a sweet, gentle boy, more like my son Tommy than my other little hellions. He fit in great with our three youngsters, and we enjoyed a few occasions together at the beach, park, and other places.

During a business trip to New York City, where Bob and his family lived, I wrapped up my business late one afternoon and began to get excited about the Neil Young concert Bob and I were scheduled to attend that night. I was hoping to have enough time to stop by the apartment to give Bobby and his mama a hug. It wasn't really odd that Bob had not communicated at all during the day; among his closest friends he's legendary for being the most perplexing communicator any of us know. He's also infamous for pulling disappearing acts during group gatherings, among other idiosyncrasies that have diminished little in later years. We all came to accept that Bob would only talk when Bob felt like talking, which except when in person wasn't too often. On this day it was getting close to concert time, and I finally called his office. His secretary had a concerned tone in her voice, putting me through a series of questions before finally telling me I needed to call his apartment. Whoever answered, presumably a relative, gave me heart-stopping news.

"Bob's at the hospital," he said. "His son is in ICU."

After finding out which hospital, I raced over by taxi. The scene in the family waiting room was surreal and far beyond my worst expectations. When I entered, still having no clue of what had transpired, I saw both Bob's mother and mother-in-law clutching rosary beads and chanting Hail Marys. While I knew both of them fairly well by this point, they barely acknowledged my presence as they continued their chants in a trancelike state. After what seemed like an eternity, Bob's wife entered the room, hugged me, and began to cry.

Little Bobby, just shy of his fourth birthday, had a few days earlier caught a stomach bug, common for a day-care-age youngster a few months away from the germ-rich world of kindergarten. With the normal advice any parent has heard from their kid's doctor, Bobby's doctor told them it was a "virus that would run its course and to drink plenty of fluids."

The next morning he stopped breathing at the breakfast table after telling his parents his legs hurt. The paramedics reached Bob about half a block from his apartment as he was sprinting toward the hospital with his lifeless son in his arms. They managed to revive Bobby, but he was in a coma. After a few days on life support, Bobby passed.

The aftermath for my heartbroken friend and his wife was not that unusual, given that individuals rarely grieve or process tragedy the same way. Their marriage did not survive, and ultimately his ex-wife unfairly decided that somehow Bob was to blame, vindictively making things even worse for him during the divorce.

For his part, Bob retreated and focused on work. Aside from his closest friends and colleagues, he lived quietly and in relative solitude for the next few years. While his generous nature, sarcastic wit, and adventurous personality returned, the scars remain. It's impossible for anyone who hasn't experienced the loss of a child to truly fathom the depth of despair this brings.

When Tommy's endless saga would bring me to my knees, I'd reflect on what my best friend had gone through and try to regain perspective. Tommy's girlfriend Missy, the latest female to fall for his pretty eyes and convincing lies, bonded with Mary. They texted and spoke frequently. It was as if they'd become candy stripers (like the World War II nurses tending to wounded soldiers) with the shared purpose of healing my son.

But their efforts became nauseating to me, given my present state of mind. While I appreciated Missy as a well-intentioned young woman with a caring heart, she was clearly as broken as my son and somehow too saccharine for my liking. Meanwhile, it seemed that my wife was back in denial, simply refusing to admit that she couldn't fix a son who had already used up his nine lives and more. I felt disgusted and couldn't stand to be around either one of them.

Tommy continued to fantasize about being a normal kid. I'd simply had enough with all of the drama and utter nonsense. Increasingly I sought refuge at my local pub and elsewhere, secretly beginning to wonder if I might be falling prey to the type of dependency that had cursed the lives of my father, brother, and son. During this period we experienced a few visits from our son's probation officer, who was content to stay in the driveway thanks to the deep barking of Barry's rambunctious and massive Chesapeake Bay retriever. I was thankful for the probation officer's fear since it ensured the interactions were short.

It's hard to imagine how difficult it would be to go through the trials and tribulations of an addict child alone, as so many single parents have. Mary and I had again shifted roles, she becoming the nurturing parent and me the tough-love father. There are many ups and downs in a thirty-two-year marriage, and I'm proud we've managed thus far to weather the issues related to our family. But the sands continue to shift, and tension between us seems always just beneath the surface. At least for now we're on the same page.

While we shouldn't have been surprised that Tommy's typical pattern would continue, his next eviction from our home was particularly gut-wrenching. A few days before his third failed rehab attempt in South Florida, Missy called Mary one night in a panic. She was with our son who could not stop crying and spoke about killing himself. What triggered his self-loathing was unknown, but we suspected he'd slipped. Missy convinced him to come home and the four of us sat around our living room, Tommy continuing to sob uncontrollably about his worthless life and the other three of us trying to console him and give him reasons to live. On the one hand, it was encouraging to see that he was feeling emotions again as compared to the robot-like state he seemed to be in when in the grasp of his preferred drug. But on the other hand, we wondered if the breakdown was severe enough that we should consider psychiatric options. Many tears were shed and hugs exchanged, and he finally fell asleep on the couch, completely spent. For the first time we considered him capable of taking his own life. At the same time, there wasn't a thing we could do.

The Baker and Marchman Acts, Florida laws created to protect despondent or mentally ill individuals from themselves, were short-term Band-Aids for a situation like our son's. Lasting only three to five days, they were quick-fix bridges to tremendously expensive long-term solutions. By now well over six figures in debt and having been through about a dozen aborted rehab attempts, throwing more money at the problem was neither logical nor possible.

Tommy seemed much better the next day, and we foolishly convinced ourselves that we'd all gotten through to him and the acute crisis was over. A day or two later, he still seemed fine and just after lunch told me he was going to take a shower. Minutes later the doorbell rang and it was his girlfriend, again in a state of panic.

"Where's Tommy?" she gasped.

"He's in the shower," I responded. "Come in."

"He's essentially been texting me good-bye," she said. "I'm worried he's going to hurt himself."

My heart racing, I ran to his bedroom door, which was locked. I could hear the shower running. Rushing to his brother's room on the other side of the Jack and Jill bathroom, I found that door was also locked. Panicking, I sprinted across the house to retrieve the doorknob center-hole key and soon managed to get his door unlocked. By now I was certain that he'd be lying there, perhaps in a pool of blood, perhaps with a needle sticking out of his arm.

Instead he was gone, along with the expensive laptop we'd recently bought to help him resume his graphic arts studies. The window to the bathroom was open, the screen taken out. Turning off the shower, which he'd left running as a diversion, my terror turned to anger. His girlfriend left in tears, and I hugged her, thanking her for how hard she'd tried to help my miserable son.

Returning like the Hulk to the rage that was then the bane of my existence, I jumped in my car and sped to the neighborhood where his favorite pawnshop was located and stormed inside. People stood back and steered clear, waiting to see the confrontation that was clearly about to come.

First I lied, saying my name was Tommy, and I'd returned to reclaim my pawned items.

"Driver's license," the slimy twenty-something employee behind the counter ordered. After I produced it and he said the number didn't match the record, my anger boiled over into a full verbal assault.

"My druggie son just stole my laptop, and I need it back," I demanded.

"Sorry, you have to wait twenty days, and then if he doesn't claim it, you can have a chance to buy it back," he sneered.

"Listen, you jackass, it's my damn laptop and I want it now!"

"Look mister, it's the law, and I don't make the law; I can't give it to you," he replied.

"Real nice business you have here, preying on drug addicts and stolen merchandise," I yelled, now in full out-of-control rage like I hadn't experienced since New Jersey about two years earlier. As I stormed out, still cursing at the pawnshop's employees and the onlookers who dared to stare at the raving lunatic stampeding back toward his car, it hit me that I was right back at the beginning of the recurring nightmare.

"Will this ever end?" I asked myself.

Later that night, with the money received from pawning the computer and cell phone, Tommy bought and ingested a huge amount of heroin in an attempt to kill himself.

16

BEYOND TWELVE STEPS:
THE BUSINESS
OF RECOVERY

As Tommy's battle continued to wreak havoc on our marriage, family, and health, I resumed weekly sessions with my therapist. The topic was almost always Tommy. Mary had gone on a health kick, lost weight, and was eating the healthiest she had in her life. My daughter and I continued to struggle.

My therapist, David, is a former professional tennis player from Australia who has an easygoing, yet no-nonsense demeanor that I definitely need. Once skeptical, perhaps from years working as a journalist, I by now had become cynical, particularly relating to psychiatrists, psychologists, and therapists. Tommy's journey had run us through a gauntlet of them, and most seemed only a step or two removed from televangelists. "Come and see the light of recovery!" was often the refrain. "Now that will be $200."

David is different, and we connected nearly immediately. Our earliest sessions, which in my mind were to help navigate through a bumpy time in my career, soon shifted to my relationship with my father. Before too long I found myself confronting deep feelings of rejection and isolation dating back to my tumultuous childhood and opening up black holes in my memory that I'd blocked as a way to cope. In retrospect, these sessions likely prepared me for the parental challenges ahead. Over time—including the life-changing act of forgiving my father for his transgressions and absence during most of my childhood, only a few short years before his death—I was able to shed much of the self-pity and insecurity that had dogged me for years.

Now, about seven years later and after months of not seeing him, David and I sat down to catch up. For the next few years, the topic usually was Tommy.

"I'm angry again and blaming myself," I said.

"You and Mary are doing the best you can," he replied. "I admire how much you are willing to get down in the trenches, fight hard to save him, and never give up."

"I spent too much time on my other sons because I love sports; I should have been there more and gone on camping trips with him instead of coaching so many baseball and basketball teams."

"You can't blame yourself. There's no handbook for parenting, and you're far from alone. He must know you love him. Even the struggles you're going through now are a clear signal to him how important he is. You've just got to keep him afloat, keeping his head above water. You're doing a great job."

By the time Mary and I had become de facto experts in the science and business of recovery, thanks to the growing number of our son's relapses, we began to question the conventional wisdom that twelve-step programs are the one and only way a person can get clean and lead a productive life. This was presented as established fact by every recovery program and addiction specialist we had met, including my twenty-five-plus-year clean and sober brother. It was all or nothing, according to leaders in the "rooms."

After surviving seven years and over a dozen failed recovery attempts by Tommy, including residential treatment, outpatient programs, AA and NA meetings, and just about every other potential option, all with virtually no success, I began to have doubts about this all-or-nothing approach, particularly where opioid addicts are concerned. If total abstinence is the only answer, why does this approach seem to rarely work with opioid users?

It's a topic David and I wrestled with at one of our sessions. He shared my skepticism.

"It works for some, but not everyone," he said.

"Exactly. Like my brother," I replied. "I'm not knocking a program that has helped so many people. But we live in a gray world, and few things are that black and white."

A music fanatic, I'd read and listened to Howard Stern interviews with several musicians who had overcome drug addictions. Greg Allman's testimony was particularly encouraging given Tommy's track record; it had taken Allman fourteen rehabs before he successfully beat back heroin and alcohol dependency. Maybe there was hope for Tommy, I thought.

Each musician had a different story on how they had escaped the powerful and destructive forces of their addiction.

Some, such as James Taylor, had worked the twelve steps, accepted a higher power, and never touched a drink or drug again. Others, like David Crosby, had put down hard drugs years earlier but continued to smoke pot or drink moderately without experiencing a relapse. Stern always challenged such claims and dug deeper, but each subject's answers made sense from my perspective. One size doesn't fit all.

"Hey, it's a deeply personal thing, and what works for one person doesn't necessarily work for another," responded one rock musician. "We don't all share the same body chemistry, spiritual beliefs, or life experiences."

Overall, twelve-step programs still seem relatively sound to me, at least for the structure and shared camaraderie they can provide. But to assume that a program designed for alcoholics more than half a century ago is the one and only way an opioid user can possibly overcome their dependency seems illogical to me at this point. My younger brother beat the odds by getting clean and staying clean for over two decades after a single thirty-day rehab program. But countless others fail. Stats in the complex cesspool of addiction are so hard to track that trying to pinpoint success rates is futile. Most addicts yo-yo in and out of various programs frequently, making any progress nearly impossible to scientifically measure.

We recognized early on that one of Tommy's key issues seemed to be a lack of faith in a higher power. Despite having been raised in a Christian household, he did not believe in God, Jesus, or any organized religion. We discussed this numerous times and I personally found it distressing. But there was much more to his struggles than lack of faith or the chemical dependencies he established while numbing his personal pain. The drug use was a result, not the root cause, of whatever thoughts decimated his self-esteem. Opiate use was a symptom, not the disease itself—a self-medicating way to escape his inner torment.

As the cycle of despair continued, with no positive results, my view shifted from viewing addiction as something that might be cured through committed abstinence to something that was far more rooted in a person's psychological and psychiatric well being. Individual brain chemistry, which clearly can be rewired through substance abuse, seems to have as much, if not more, to do with the inability of an addict to break free as other causes. How could there be just one solution to such a complex problem? Why are some people able to shake off opiates forever but continue to drink or smoke in moderation? How did my late father, who never attended a single AA meeting or read a single word from AA's *The Big Book*, simply decide to stop drinking one day at fifty-something years old and live another two decades without taking another sip of alcohol? Or how do you explain my son, who was exposed to so much recovery doctrine over a five-year period that he could teach it, yet continued to relapse time after time? Life is gray, not black and white. There is no silver bullet.

There are also no perfect answers when it comes to matters of the brain; after all, it's the final frontier in medical science. What I've grown to believe is that substance abuse stems from a complex combination of brain chemistry, genetic predisposition, socialization, and life experiences. Often it is inextricably linked with mental imbalances such as bipolar disorder, social anxiety, or depression.

In the throes of crisis, you sometimes hear only what you want to hear, and Mary and I harbored secret envy of parents who reported that their kids were doing better while Tommy continued to flail. Bumping into some of these same parents months or years later, we realized they were mostly in the same boat. As Tommy's vicious cycle of relapse and recovery continued, we clung to the only bright spot we could find— the time between relapses and Tommy's desire to get clean kept getting shorter. Instead of descending into prolonged periods of oblivion, when we might not hear from him for weeks, he seemed to nearly immediately call for help just a day or two after falling off the wagon.

When we received our son's collect call, we were not that surprised. Less than a week after we had visited him in his latest halfway house and listened to him ramble on about aliens, conspiracy theories, and other subjects, our son was arrested, this time for possession of a controlled substance. He swore he had been only seeking to make a few bucks by agreeing to buy dope for a roommate. He was booked into the Palm Beach County Jail for violating probation. While the possession charges were dropped within two days, the inefficiencies inherent in our overcrowded jail and prison bureaucracy left him behind bars for the next two months, which was fine with us. Basically the two Florida counties couldn't get their act together on a transfer back to our home county, where he had been under probation.

A sad and well-documented travesty tracing back to America's war on drugs has been the harsh sentences handed out for relatively nonviolent drug offenses, a major contributor to the overcrowding that plagues our nation's penal system today. It's a war that, despite popular belief largely due to Nancy Reagan's highly visible "Just Say No" campaign, was not started by Ronald Reagan but was launched by Richard Nixon as a way to get back at the antiwar protestors chanting outside his White House doors. Every year between 1993 and 2009, more people were sentenced to state and federal prison due to drug crimes than violent crimes. Since 2000, one-third of all convictions have been related to drug crimes, more during this period than for property crimes. Of the thirty million drug arrests and subsequent incarcerations that occurred between 1993 and 2011, twenty-four million of them were for possessing drugs, not selling them.[1] Prison overcrowding, including the disproportionate number of minorities behind bars, remains a very complex issue, and there are far more societal issues at play than the war on drugs. Yet the ease with which a nonviolent drug user can be locked up, often for long periods of time, is alarming.

With Tommy behind bars, I stayed a day longer on a business trip in the area to see him on a Saturday morning, one of only two mornings per week when visitors were allowed. The process felt odd, beginning with the parking lot signs to leave all cell phones, weapons, and contraband in your vehicle before entering the wire-mesh walkway toward the jail's rear entrance door. After the expected metal detector screening and a series of electronic double-security doors, deputies ushered the visitors into a waiting room. I was sad to see how many young children were there, waiting to see their incarcerated fathers.

When we finally were ushered through the last step of security by a no-nonsense deputy, we were directed into a stark, fluorescent-lit visiting area featuring the two-way Plexiglas windows and phones common in movies and TV shows. As I chose my tiny, attached metal stool next to a phone, one of about fifteen to twenty available, I saw the woman next to me pull a wet wipe from her purse and wipe down the phone. Now disgusted with the idea of putting the receiver against my ear and the bottom part near my mouth, I improvised using my T-shirt.

We were all positioned around the perimeter of the inner bullpen as guards ushered a big group of inmates inside, each locating his visitor and moving to the stool across from him or her. Face to face but separated by Plexiglas, it was a sad scene. Young kids cried, asking when Daddy would be coming home. Older kids shuffled awkwardly behind their mothers and younger siblings, looking as if this was the last place they wanted to be. Mothers discussed money and other problems. It struck me how privileged my children had been compared to most of these kids. But addiction is an equal-opportunity problem that couldn't care less about economic or family circumstances.

Tommy was one of the last to enter, and he had a large brown Afro that made him look somewhat crazed. He looked more like Cheech Marin of Cheech and Chong fame than the son I had visualized in my mind that morning.

"Hi, Dad," he said after picking up the black phone. "Why are you here?"

"Not to bail you out," I answered. "What happened?"

"I needed money and agreed to score this guy in the house some dope," he said, continuing to insist he wasn't using at the time.

"Where's all your stuff?" I asked.

"It's probably gone. The woman running the halfway house is not a good person, and she probably has sold it by now. The cops wouldn't let me go back and get anything."

His look was sullen and distant. Despite my best efforts, he barely managed a slight smile. After about fifteen minutes, an announcement was made to wrap up conversations, and the visit ended as abruptly as it began. As I watched him walk out of the room alongside much larger, scarier-looking inmates, it felt unreal that this was once my sweet little boy.

In one of many futile attempts at recovering Tommy's possessions from pawnshops, drug dealer residences, or halfway houses, I soon was pounding on the door of the house. The slovenly lady who answered allowed me to step inside briefly but said there was nothing of his there.

"I have no idea what is even his," she said. "Kids are in and out of here all the time, and we get new kids every week."

Halfway houses are simply another cog in the recovery industry, an alternative to sleeping on the streets but barely. Like in NA meetings and rehab centers, there are many addicts in halfway houses to gravitate toward if a person is not interested in trying to get clean. Most houses do not allow locks on bedroom doors, leading to constant theft and strife among the residents. During periods when Tommy found jobs and tried to get on track, he'd sometimes come home to a halfway house after work to find his money or belongings gone from under his mattress or dresser drawer. This usually led to angry accusations, getting kicked out, or simply giving up. Relapse was nearly certain to follow.

After a few more weeks, which were likely agonizing for him but a welcome stretch of calm for us, Tommy was transferred to the jail in our home county. My wife visited once, but I refused. During this period we took solace in the fact that he was at least clean and alive. Or so we thought. Tommy later told me that it was quite easy to get drugs in jail if you had something to trade, such as cigarettes or money. He said they passed the time with dice and card games, gambling for cigarettes.

A few weeks after being returned to the county jail in our area, Tommy's day in court finally arrived, and we drove downtown to attend. His was the very last case called by the judge, meaning we were treated to a full three hours of watching other inmates and their lawyers, one by one, shuffle slowly through the obviously broken system. Many cases were dismissed due to errors in processing or because the clogged penal bureaucracy had already resulted in jail terms longer than the judge would have ordered. Other more violent offenders only said, "Yes, ma'am," and their public defendants did all the talking.

One by one the judge cycled through the morning caseload, taking a twenty-minute break at one point. The family holding room on the other side of glass from the court chambers had a small area about the size of a phone booth in which a family member was allowed to step up to and ask questions through an intercom. The room was packed when we arrived at 8:00 a.m., but now approaching the lunch hour, it was completely empty except for Mary, an armed deputy, and me. Finally our son was brought in front of the judge. Peering out from under a huge, bushy fro, his brown hair matted and filthy looking, Tommy spotted us on the other side of the glass and gave us a nod. He looked ashamed and embarrassed, which was better than the dispassionate, glazed look I'd seen far too many times before.

With his parents unwilling to pump any more money into his bottomless pit to hire a lawyer, he appeared on his own accord. When the judge realized how much time he'd already spent in jail due to the inept coordination between two different counties, she dismissed the violation and released him. For the first time in two months, Tommy was no longer behind bars.

17

BACK TO THE BRINK

After giving his girlfriend, Missy, and me the slip using the running-shower trick and then pawning his new laptop to afford a lethal amount of synthetic heroin, Tommy had returned to the house of his bloated drug dealer to try to permanently end his pain. Just two days after the sobbing episode in our living room that had terrified his girlfriend and parents, he shot up an enormous amount of drugs in an effort to pass out and never wake up again. He succeeded, briefly.

When he stopped breathing, the enormous man who had sold him the stuff and who owned the house performed CPR on Tommy and brought him back.

"You're not going to die in my house, mofo!" he told Tommy once he had been revived. "Go somewhere else to die," he ordered, showing the level of concern drug dealers truly have for their customers.

Tommy called Missy, who mobilized Mary, and within hours they'd managed to pick him up from a neighborhood she later described as "very scary." Missy convinced him to enter the hospital to detox. Sadly, there was to be a third time we would process through this hospital's emergency room, only to learn that the facility no longer accepted detox patients due to a change in medical laws.

A few days later Missy drove him from the hospital to a treatment facility an hour north of Orlando, a place that was relatively new and had earned a good reputation. This time we did not participate beyond continuing to keep Tommy on our family's insurance plan. It was entirely through Missy's efforts that he was given another chance at recovery. Any costs that our insurance didn't cover were his problem, not ours, we decided. Mary kept tabs on the situation through Missy, and we also spoke to our son a few times on the phone and tried to be encouraging.

Once the amount of time that insurance would cover ran out, the center of course determined that either we would have to pay privately or he would have to leave. Coincidentally, it was the day before Thanksgiving. We reluctantly decided to bring him back home to see his family for the holiday.

After his second death-by-overdose attempt, my attitude toward him began to shift. Again Mary and I reversed roles. This time she had simply had enough and felt completely betrayed by him after trying so hard to get him on track. She was finished, except for the deep love and hope she still harbored and the intense worry only a mother can truly understand. I felt the tremendous sadness and hopelessness, wondering if there was anything we would ever be able to do to help our son.

Tommy looked and sounded great during the holiday; extended sobriety apparently had cleared some of the cobwebs from his damaged brain. We decided to let him stay home through Christmas to give us time, for a change, to consider future options without the pressure of a twenty-four-hour deadline.

In a somewhat surreal experience a couple weeks later, Mary and Jessie were driving back into our neighborhood when Mary spotted Tommy's stolen car in our neighborhood, the second automobile appropriated by drug dealers over money Tommy owed them. Mary again decided to throw caution to the wind and now was tailing his car just a few blocks from our home. An aggressive woman who rarely lets go of anything without a fight, she was determined to recover this car as well. It was a wild coincidence that she had spotted it at all, since the drug dealer lived twenty miles away in a different city.

The driver didn't notice that a diminutive suburban mom with a Christmas tree on her roof rack was tailing him, a feisty lady who wasn't thinking about the potential danger of confronting the driver.

When he parked at a house and went inside, she drove around the corner where she could keep a sight line and called the local police chief. By the time the driver came back outside, two uniformed officers greeted him. Since we had yet to file a stolen vehicle report, the driver was released. Our son's car was retrieved and eventually sold for much less than he'd paid for it just months before.

Tommy again decided that he needed to leave Orlando before slipping back into his old ways. He seemed to hate the merry-go-round he'd been riding and was sincere in his desire to start fresh somewhere else.

Our son Paul, back from working in Seattle and now living in Tampa, began talking with Tommy about moving there. Paul made it clear that living with him was not an option, so the two of them began seeking halfway houses that weren't far from where Paul lived. Despite separate conversations with both his parents about what a foolish idea we thought it would be to disrupt his life by bringing his addicted brother into it, just like his grandmother Dona did before him, Paul ignored our warnings. Soon we found ourselves setting Tommy up in his fifth halfway house, this one owned by a married couple, themselves recovering addicts. At first the woman seemed to truly care about the lost souls paying a significant sum each week, most courtesy of their parents, to rent a room. The renters were encouraged to attend meetings. In time we would find out that her concern was an act, just another elaborate lie in the deceptive culture of drugs and the recovery business.

For several weeks, Tommy seemed to finally be moving in the right direction, landing a job as a lead cook at a new restaurant that opened just blocks from his house. The general manager loved him and the gregarious regional manager, whom I'd known for a few years, took him under his wing. For the next several weeks he worked overtime at the job, which experienced a strong opening and much higher than expected sales. Our family visited him on friends-and-family night, and he beamed with pride when introducing us to colleagues.

Unfortunately the other cook that Tommy was splitting most of the duties of running the kitchen with was injured in a motorcycle accident and had to take a leave of absence. Tommy suddenly found himself working sixty hours a week, sometimes twelve hours straight, something he was neither physically nor mentally ready to do. Never saying no to taking on double shifts or coming in on his day off, he drove

174

himself to exhaustion. Faced with this new type of adversity and because of his longing to be normal, which included smoking weed behind the restaurant or at parties with his coworkers, he soon slipped back into opiate use.

Paul noticed it too and came to the realization that having his brother living nearby had become burdensome. Tommy began showing up to work late and, on at least one occasion, high. Within a matter of days Tommy went from being the star kitchen employee of this busy new restaurant to being fired. The slide down was always fast.

By now the halfway house ruse being carried out by the woman who ran the house became evident to us all. A couple weeks earlier on a Friday evening, we pulled into the parking lot adjacent to the halfway house to pick Tommy up to take him to dinner. The woman sprang off the front porch when she saw my car and rushed to the driver's window, moving much more quickly than I'd thought possible. She was anxious to collect that week's rent. I immediately recognized the familiar look of desperate angst in her eyes, an anxious stare we knew from experience was that of an addict craving a fix. Tommy had told us she was using, but we no longer believed anything he said so had dismissed his claim as paranoia. Adding to his anger and growing spiral downward was the fact that other halfway house residents were routinely stealing from him. Despite his constant protests, the sloppy, deceptive house manager refused to let him put a lock on his door. We agreed that he needed to move on and that the relatively expensive house in the decrepit neighborhood was doing more harm than good.

Before we could find an alternative, his disgust with the woman escalated to such a point that he took video footage on his phone to prove she was using. He planned to report the couple to the police and provide the video as evidence. Once she caught him filming, an argument ensued, and he was kicked out of the house. A far-too-familiar cycle began once again.

For a couple days he slept at a new girlfriend's place until her mother put an end to that. He spent other nights at no-tell motels with fifteen-dollar-a-night rooms, good for an hour or the entire night. For all his lack of common sense, retarded social development, and psychological struggles, he certainly was resilient. But it didn't take long between food, lodging, and presumably drugs for him to run out of money and again call home tearful and defeated.

It was clear he was using again, but we couldn't bear the thought of him back on the streets. I purchased him a train ticket back to Orlando. He missed the train of course, no longer having a car, so we called Paul, the brother who had coaxed him to Tampa with the best of intentions. By now, however, Paul was fed up.

"He can't stay here," he said.

"But he has nowhere else to go; he missed his train, and there are thunderstorms tonight. Can't he just crash on your couch a couple nights until we can help him figure out what's next?"

"No way, Dad, I don't trust him," Paul replied. "I have my friend's expensive guitar and other valuable items here, and I'm not going to risk it."

"Listen, you self-centered prima donna," I responded, anger rising in my voice. "You're the one who wanted him there in the first place; we tried to warn you what would happen. And now you can't even let him sleep on your couch!"

"Screw you, Dad, I'm not doing it," he said, hanging up on me.

While Paul kept his word about not letting Tommy inside his rented bungalow, he did go pick him up and let him pitch a tent in his tiny side yard. He also let him shower inside the next morning. Paul, now experiencing the conflicting emotions of having failed to help his brother and probably feeling he'd been duped, was discouraged.

"None of us can do anything," Paul said. "He has to do it for himself. You have to stop rescuing him and just let go."

While I knew he was right, knowing and doing remained two different things in our household. We let him come home again.

18

BREAKTHROUGH

As I painfully hobbled my way toward the hospital elevators that would lift me to Tommy's floor, my swollen knee was throbbing. Walking briskly around a corner in my house earlier that morning, I had been blindsided by my son's rambunctious, 105-pound retriever with a full head of steam running to greet me. I never saw him coming, and his full body weight sideswiped me at knee level like a linebacker unleashing a full speed hit on a running back. Both my knees buckled, and I crumpled to the tile floor in pain.

The physical pain was nothing compared to the mental pain Tommy's latest fall had instantaneously created. When I got to his hospital room, I could see he was hooked up to an IV with heart monitoring wires spread across his chest. At first I was relieved not to find him bloodied and battered. But the relief soon turned to frustration, and then anger, when he would not admit to me what had occurred and the familiar lying began.

"What happened, son?" I demanded.

"I'm not sure; I blacked out and woke up here," he replied. "But I feel fine and need to get to work, and the nurses are giving me a hard time about leaving."

"Where is your scooter?" I asked, concerned about his only mode of transportation, given that he had managed to squander two different cars. He also had paid us back about only $200 so far of the $1,500 purchase price.

"I don't know."

"What do you mean you don't know?" I asked.

By now I was certain Tommy had relapsed and was hiding something from me. This was further confirmed when I tried to get any information from the nurse.

"It's up to him to share any information with you. I'm legally prevented from telling you anything unless he grants me permission."

Irritated with the runaround I was getting, I asked my son to grant that permission. He declined. It was clear from his cranky and nasty demeanor, now resurfacing after lying dormant for months, that he had relapsed. He told me nothing.

"What is going on?" I asked, my voice rising.

"Get out of my room," Tommy barked at me, then shouted to the nurse, "I don't want him here, he's stressing me out!"

"You're on your own," I told him, storming out of the unit as fast as my gimpy legs would carry me. My mind racing, I paused in the lobby just before exiting the hospital doors and decided I simply could not accept this turn of events. Stubbornly I turned around and headed back for the elevators. This time a pair of security guards were waiting for me outside Tommy's room, ready to physically block me from entering.

"Did my son commit a crime?" I asked.

"Sir, you need to keep your voice down," a nurse said, scolding me for potentially disturbing other patients who might be resting.

"No," said one of the security guards, "we're here to make sure he doesn't leave."

Still with no answers, but on the verge of getting myself into trouble, I hobbled away. For once I practiced self-restraint in the desperate chaos of my son's struggle.

Tommy had not come home the previous night, the same day he had rear-ended a car while driving my truck. He never borrowed my SUV and was much more accustomed to driving his mother's car, but because she was working and an afternoon thunderstorm was rolling in, I offered to let him take it.

"Remember, Tommy," I said, in what turned out to be a prophetic warning. "My truck is a lot heavier and older than Mom's, so it takes a lot longer to stop. Be careful."

Less than two hours later he slid on the wet streets into the back of a car he'd been following too closely. Thankfully, he was completely sober. Sadly, it triggered the worst of his self-loathing and another relapse that almost killed him.

He was despondent when he returned home with my truck's grill destroyed, headlight smashed, hood crumpled up, and bumper hanging by a thread.

"I'm so sorry, Dad," he said, looking like he was about to cry.

"What happened?" I asked, not doing a good job at hiding my disgust.

"It wasn't my fault; she stopped short, and I went into her."

"I can't talk to you right now," I said, walking away.

Despite years of practice, I still had difficulty accepting such setbacks with grace or patience. This time I was able to refrain from articulating the unkind thoughts popping into my mind at the moment and had enough control to try to calm down. A lousy poker player, my emotions were easy to read. My attempt to separate before saying something I'd regret wasn't enough for my son though, who followed me into our bedroom, badgering me to talk about it.

"Enough. I said I don't want to talk about it now," I shouted.

As he hung his head and walked away in shame, I immediately felt remorseful. I went down to his room to talk.

"Look, son, I'm really sorry I just yelled at you. I'm pissed about the situation, not pissed at you," I said. "A car is just a material thing, and it's why we have insurance; it will be fixed. The main thing is that you're okay and that no one was hurt."

Despite this backtracking, Tommy fixated on my immediate reaction. I asked him to spend time together that night, but he said he had plans to go out with a friend. I begged him to come with me and not take his scooter out that rainy night, but his mind was made up.

Before he left I again told him how much I loved him and how glad we were that he hadn't been hurt. I repeated my statement about the truck being a material thing that would simply be fixed and wouldn't cost much due to insurance.

"I'm sorry I let you down again, Dad," was all he said. "I love you too."

We didn't hear from him again until he woke up in the hospital the next day and called Mary.

It turned out that he had attended a party on Cinco de Mayo, which like St. Patrick's Day is a holiday mostly used as an excuse for people to over-drink. He ran into an old accomplice at the party who happened to have just what Tommy was looking for to escape from his feelings of worthlessness. On the way home, high on whatever combination of alcohol and drugs he ingested that night, he managed to guide his scooter into a 7-Eleven parking spot because he had to go to the bathroom and wanted a bottle of water. Miraculously, the moment he blacked out occurred on the sidewalk outside the convenience store rather than behind the wheel of his scooter.

He was rushed to the hospital by ambulance and, according to the emergency room doctor, was barely breathing. The reason for the mystery surrounding my visit the next day was that the doctor had ordered him committed to the hospital for a minimum of three days of evaluation under a Florida law designed to protect people who were a danger to themselves or others. The doctor later told us that especially when consumed with alcohol, the combination of drugs he had taken was lethal. She said that he was very lucky to be alive.

The spiral downward was rapid after he was released from the hospital. Breaking the promise to rest for a few days before returning to work, he pressured the doctor to sign a release form, and he was back in the restaurant's kitchen within three days.

Professional rationalizers by this point, Mary and I convinced ourselves that it was the best thing for him and that lying around the house worrying that he'd lose the job he loved would only make him more depressed.

Previously I'd convinced Mary to try a new approach. We were both so worn down that we felt there was nothing to lose. The one thing we agreed on was that under no circumstances were we going to throw any more money at the expensive recovery machine. Our love and desperation overshadowed our better judgment, as it had so many times before.

Our children thought we were nuts.

"What the heck are you guys thinking?" our other two sons asked, each in their own ways. "Hasn't he done enough to hurt you already?"

Tommy's siblings had long ago become fed up with his up-and-down routine and although they all still loved him, they had erected much stronger boundaries than we were capable of. Ever since the deliberate overdose and despair that led up to it, I'd begun looking at our son's addiction from a different perspective. No program, residential or outpatient, series of meetings, or halfway houses had worked. The only thing that kept him alive was the love of his family and the fact that we wouldn't give up on him. He later confirmed this multiple times. Since Mary and I were now in a stronger place mentally and physically, we decided to try a different approach. Virtually all other options had been exhausted except for sending him back to the streets homeless and broke, which we couldn't bring ourselves to do again. So we let him move back in.

He was very frail and emotionally shattered. His only chance was to stay off the hard drugs and heal in a loving environment, we reasoned. As always, his younger sister was delighted to see him and greeted him with great enthusiasm and affection, even though she remained cautious. Over the next few days Tommy cleaned up his appearance, getting a haircut, having a pierced stud removed from his cheek, and shaving off his beard. He looked good for the first time in many months, and before long his smile began to reappear, especially when he was clowning around with his sweet little sister.

We even went along with the idea he'd long held on to that just because he had a beer or smoked a little weed once in a while didn't mean he'd return to hard drugs. As my therapist, who affirmed our decision, put it, "You're just trying to keep his head above water."

It felt liberating to consider a different approach that wasn't so rigid, and I even treated myself to the slight hope that he could fully recover. The approach seemed to be working great at first. One night I even took Tommy, now twenty-two, to a local Irish pub where I play on a steel-tip darts team and introduced him to several friends. For the first time ever, I also had a drink with my son.

This simple act made a huge, unexpected impact in our relationship. It was like an invisible wall between us had suddenly dissolved, and he seemed as happy that night as I'd ever seen him since childhood. It hit me like a ton of bricks. More than anything, Tommy needed my unconditional acceptance!

Mary had been saying for some time, "He needs his father."

As much as I inherently knew this, it was tremendously difficult to spend time with him while he was using. In my initial belief in the all-or-nothing doctrine of twelve-step recovery, I thought that even having a single drink with him would be contributing to what most experts still consider a disease.

But now the dramatic change in his behavior and the joy in his smile made it obvious that what he needed was not just my love but also my acceptance. How could I not have seen this earlier, having grown up with a father who preferred to spend time alone rather than with his family? Having grown up feeling rejected by a father who didn't have a full-time job but still couldn't find time to attend even one of my countless sporting events or concerts, I knew the pain of indifference as well as anyone. In this moment of clarity, I changed. From that night and every day since, I treated Tommy as my adult son and fully accepted his unique viewpoints, clothes, and grooming preferences. I no longer viewed him as a pinless grenade that could explode at any moment. He sensed this shift and was elated.

On the way home the night we shared our first drink, he asked if I wanted to perhaps pick up some cigars to share so we could continue the one-on-one conversation and father-son bonding at home. We stopped by a store to pick up two stogies and proceeded to sit next to our pool, music in the background, and talk for hours. It was a new beginning in our relationship, and while my son was still far from out of the woods regarding his drug problem, we began to look forward, not back.

When I'd taken my father on a ride back to the farm of my youth during my final visit to his home, for the first time I understood things from his perspective and how hard life had been on him. In fully opening the communication channels with my son that night, I felt an eerie similarity. Once I stopped looking at Tommy as someone whom it was my job to save, the vibe between us immediately changed. Puffing on our cigars and enjoying the cool, breezy break in the hot weather that night, we had the most honest and open dialogue we'd ever shared.

I learned how he first got into drugs and how things had progressed, things he'd shared with others during various recovery attempts but was too ashamed to tell us. As if hearing everything through a fresh set of ears, I got a much better sense of where he'd been, how he was now feeling, and the triggers that led to his repeated relapses. I got to know my son far better that night and the following few days than I had over the previous five years. For the first time, I shared with him some of my own shortcomings and father issues. I honestly answered his questions about which drugs I'd experimented with during my college years. We were completely open and honest with each other, and if he asked me a question, I responded directly and truthfully.

It dawned on me during the next few days of reflecting and discussing this breakthrough with my wife, closest friends, and therapist that my full acceptance was more important to Tommy than anything else. All he wanted was to spend time with me and have me accept him for who he was.

With the communication door between us finally wide open, things went along very well for several weeks. With the exception of a slipup on Christmas Day, where our full house of relatives and friends triggered his social anxiety disorder and led to him to buy and ingest a tranquilizer pill, Tommy was functioning, happy, and getting healthier.

He found a job on his own working at an upscale but funky restaurant as a cook. He was diligent about arriving on time and the managers seemed to love him. He decided he wanted to go back to working on his degree and enrolled in classes at the local community college. He earned great grades for most of the semester, proudly showing us the tests and papers he'd written that got high marks. We felt that chalking up enough small victories would rebuild his self-esteem, and this is exactly what was happening.

As his sobriety neared 120 days, a new record, some familiar signs began to worry us. He spoke to me about his lack of friends and inability to sustain any relationships with the two or three girls he'd recently dated. Unfortunately, he'd blown up too many bridges, and even his best friend, Scott, whom Tommy had stolen from and lied to, no longer would speak to him. His work life continued to go well, as did his classes. Physically, he was back to a healthy weight and was even undergoing a treatment process to rid hepatitis C, a disease he had contracted from either drugs or tattoo needles, from his body. But with no social life, Tommy began to become depressed. We all knew Orlando was the wrong place for him to be feeling lousy about himself. All he needed was a trigger to flush the tremendous progress he'd made. The accident with my truck was the proverbial straw that broke his back.

Tommy had yet to learn how to cope with setbacks, and sadly, seemed snakebit by life. Like the sad donkey Eeyore in *Winnie the Pooh*, it was as if a black cloud followed him around. Even when he was sober, problems seemed to find him. Unfortunately, his response to any significant thing that went wrong, each of which must have been amplified in his mind, was to run back to his drug of choice.

Our new, open, and honest communication commitment survived his Cinco de Mayo debacle, and we discussed this recurring theme extensively.

"Son, life is full of ups and downs," I recall telling him. "Lots of times things suck. But every day is a new chance, and you just have to not let the bad things pull you down into a hole that you end up making deeper and deeper."

He shared with me that he just felt it would be better for everyone if he wasn't around, and he again was obsessed with his perception that he'd let me down with the auto accident.

"Our relationship is the best it has ever been," he said, "and I really felt you were beginning to trust me again. But then I screwed up and wrecked your truck. Mom and you have spent so much money on me already, and now I'm costing you more. I let you down again."

"It's a material thing and will be fixed in two or three weeks; don't worry about it," I said, trying to reassure him. "All that matters is that you didn't get hurt."

"But it happens over and over to me," he said. "I'm just tired of nothing ever going right."

"I love you, son, your family loves you, and you have made huge progress from where you were," I said. "You shouldn't give up, just like we will *never* give up on you. You have so much life ahead of you; you're a talented artist and an extremely smart and funny person. You've just got to figure out how to handle setbacks or something bad happening to you without going back to the drugs."

We went on to discuss earlier situations and how it seemed to always be a setback of some sort—such as the breakup with a girlfriend, getting into trouble, or an accident involving a skateboard, scooter, or car—that triggered each relapse. He seemed to agree that he needed to recognize this trigger and not go down the dark road whenever something went bad and that he needed better coping mechanisms.

Although we were making progress in our relationship, it didn't stop his deep and complex need to escape through opioids. Within weeks, this need created the worst nightmare either of our youngest two children had ever witnessed, and something children should never have to see.

19

DANGEROUS DEMONS RETURN

A few days after the hospital blackout episode, Mary and I were at dinner with another couple and had just ordered appetizers and a bottle of wine when Barry and Jessie began blowing up our phones with calls and texts, which we missed at first because the ringers had been silenced.

"Answer your damn phones!" read the first text I saw from my youngest son, uncharacteristically frantic and a signal that something was terribly wrong. We bolted for home.

We were greeted by a horrific scene and our worst nightmare when it came to our daughter and her favorite brother. Jessie had come home from a play rehearsal to find Tommy passed out in his room. He was slumped with his back against the headboard, head to the side, blood on the bottom of his arm, and a needle on the bed next to him. At first it wasn't clear if he was dead or alive.

Things could have been even worse except for the opportune timing of Barry and his girlfriend, Katy, being present in the house at the time. Barry had come home a day earlier for a visit from college. When Jessie collapsed on the living room sofa, sobbing uncontrollably after seeing what she thought was her brother dead from an overdose, Katy was there to console her. Having stayed with Jessie several times while we were away, she was like a big sister to our daughter. Her presence allowed Barry to tend to the dark task at hand.

He was able to awaken Tommy by shaking him and gently slapping his face, but it was apparent how out of it he was. It was clear to all of us that our new approach had failed. Unlike his previous dozen or so relapses, this time we witnessed the ugly moment of truth firsthand. Worst of all, so did our daughter and son.

The familiar clock began ticking as we scrambled to figure out next steps. Tommy was now awake, and we began systematically searching his room for drugs and needles. In an excruciating process given that our doped-out son was babbling incoherently and present throughout, we went through every drawer, every shoebox, the inside of every trophy, every shirt and pants pocket, and essentially every nook and cranny of his room. He eventually showed us all his hiding places, which included inside the puppet hand pouch in his favorite stuffed animal, a dolphin he had never been far from as a young child. Dolphins were his favorite, and he had carried Flipper with him wherever he went. Now he reached inside to pull out a baggie containing a few small vials of powder. Concealed inside a zipper pocket in his art portfolio case, which was filled with paintings and sketches, was a package of hypodermic needles. The inside band of a baseball hat stored several varieties of pills. I easily found his jar of weed in a dresser drawer.

Well-versed in the futility of trying to use logic or reason with an addict under the influence, we all let Tommy know how much we loved him and told him we'd talk in the morning. We made it clear that this would be his last night in his room, and he seemed to accept this. But then again, it was impossible to know what he really was thinking in his haywired junkie mind.

The next morning turned out nearly as bad. The plan was to take him to the only detox option we felt would work, the same hospital where he'd first gone six years earlier. As I was getting dressed and mentally preparing for the journey, one of the many catchphrases I'd learned through Nar-Anon popped up in my head: *The definition of insanity is doing the same things over and over and expecting different results.*

"Rick, can I see you?" I heard Mary call from across the house.

Now what, I thought, hoping for something minor but anticipating something worse. Before I could get there I heard the yelling.

"What do you have?" she shrieked.

"Nothing!" Tommy yelled back.

"What is in your hand?" she screamed, her shriek a combination of anger and terror.

"Leave me alone," he pleaded.

"Rick," she cried out, "he's got something."

Entering the standoff, I demanded that Tommy show us what he now clutched in his closed fist. He was desperate that we not see it, and he began to run through the bathroom into his brother's room. I was able to catch him before he bolted from the house. He screamed and cried as we wrestled, trying with almost superhuman strength to keep me from prying open his balled-up fist to see what he was hiding. After finally prying his hand open, but not before being punctured, I found he had a needle.

He was so deep in the clutches of opiates again that even on the morning he was heading to detox, less than twenty-four hours after traumatizing his sister and family, he was hoping to shoot up one more time. *What fools we have been*, I thought, *by thinking that things could be different.*

He was hysterical, hyperventilating, and begging me to just let him go. It was the most emotionally devastating conversation I had with him, and there had been many by now.

"Dad, pleeease, just let me go," he said, sobbing. "You don't deserve this; everyone would be better off if I just went my own way."

"That's not true, son; you have a problem but we're never going to give up on you," I said.

"But I'm a worthless piece of crap," he said, the tears pouring down his cheeks. "I just keep messing up over and over. I just can't get it. It's not fair to you guys."

"Tommy, you've got to stop thinking this way," I replied. "You are part of this family, every one of us loves you. The most selfish and unfair thing you could ever do to us would be to hurt yourself. You can do this, but you've got to realize that you have to commit to it and work hard at it."

"Please, Dad, just let me take some things and go," he pleaded. "I'll travel and camp and go out west."

"No, son, let's go," I said firmly. "I love you and that's why we have to go now."

We hugged and shed a lot of tears at the conclusion of this terrible morning battle. By the time we were in the car and rolling toward the hospital, he had accepted that he needed help and no longer resisted.

We signed in at the hospital's emergency room desk. Having sat in this same room for the same reason for hours on two previous trips, I was relieved that it was relatively empty on this particular Sunday morning. Now hypersensitive to his every move after having experienced every escape and con imaginable, I began to worry when he didn't come out of the hospital bathroom right away. I nervously watched the door for nearly ten minutes before breaking down and knocking on it.

"Tommy, are you okay in there?"

"Yeah," he responded, emerging less than a minute later.

I'd forgotten that he was still under the influence, nowhere near as incoherent as he was the previous night but still pretty loopy. I'd not taken into account how slow he was in this state, taking forever to complete the most mundane tasks. After about an hour, we were called and taken back to a room. Less than thirty minutes later came the bad news that the hospital no longer accepted detoxification patients.

"And you couldn't tell us that at the beginning?" I asked, exasperated. "So I wasted two hours when my son needs a place to go so you could make sure to charge me for the emergency room exam?"

"I'm sorry, sir," was the nurse's robotic reply.

Back in the car with my son, we discussed options.

"The place in Umatilla was really good," Tommy said. "The people were nice, and I did well until my insurance ran out. What about going there?"

Unfortunately, the same problem that had led to having two cars and unknown amounts of money taken from him by drug dealers made the free, public detox places in the area run by groups such as the Salvation Army too dangerous an option. He was certain he'd be spotted by someone there and reported to drug dealers he owed money to. Exhausted, we agreed that Umatilla was still the best and closest option, and we began the long, arduous process of trying to get him processed and admitted on a Sunday. First they interviewed him about his usage, and he stepped out of the car so I couldn't hear the full laundry list of everything he'd resumed using. His drug inventory was something he was clearly ashamed of, particularly when it came to his parents knowing all the gory details.

At first the person handling weekend admissions said it would be impossible to get him in until Monday. There's no way either of us could have made it that long.

"Listen, this can't wait until Monday; it's an acute crisis now," I explained. "I have to get him somewhere today."

"Okay, I'll try to reach the director and will call you back but can't promise anything," he said.

Recognizing that the sooner we got out of Orlando the better, we began heading north. We found a decent looking restaurant in an old building and stopped for lunch to kill time. Many customers were there for the Sunday brunch buffet, located adjacent to where we were seated. A few returning to the trough to refill their plates for a second or third time shot disapproving glances at my raggedy-looking, tattooed son. I restrained myself from the nasty comments I was tempted to throw out; instead I just stared each one down with the most menacing scowl I could muster.

It's interesting how much the difficult realities of addiction can remind you what really matters in life and what doesn't. When my friend Bob buried his only child unexpectedly, the experience made me rethink my priorities and career, leading to changes in both. When I first grappled with the reality of Tommy's addiction, I was embarrassed to share it with all but the closest friends and family members. Now I no longer cared what anyone thought, least of all some ignorant, judgmental crackers chowing down at a buffet.

From the time we left the hospital emergency room and throughout our lunch, we engaged in some amazing conversation and even found ourselves sharing several chuckles. The two of us had been down this road many times by now, and the day that had begun with such emotional chaos became relaxed. Even though he had relapsed, the ease with which we were now communicating was far different. *At least we have bonded over the last few months*, I thought, *and could talk openly with each other.*

Finally we got the phone call we needed. They were ready to admit him at the center. It was a good thing too because the cramps and nausea caused by opiate withdrawal were beginning to kick in. After buying him the requisite packs of cigarettes he wanted for detox, I essentially walked him in, gave them his duffel bag, hugged him good-bye, and left.

Tommy completed his detox and, as usual, did well during the first two weeks in recovery. He told me that it was the same stuff he'd been through many times before, and that one counselor said he knew so much he should be teaching the program. Everything seemed rosy, as it had in honeymoon periods past. But then they wanted to extend his program, and he balked.

We'd gotten a call from the team assigned to Tommy with the strong recommendation that he needed a program much longer than thirty days. Our son was convinced that all such programs were first and foremost about the money, a feeling I came to share over time. He felt that it would be a complete waste of money to sit in groups and cover the same ground again. My brother agreed.

"He's got a head full of NA and has all the tools already," Ron said. "He just needs to decide to do it. More rehab would be a waste of money and time."

Mary and I were also skeptical that beyond thirty days, there would not be much value. But it was his call and his choice on a path forward, something that Mary apparently forgot when she fielded a call one morning from a center employee.

"Your son is threatening to leave, and we don't think it's a good idea," the caller told Mary. "We think he needs at least another thirty to sixty days, but he's asking for his phone and wallet back to leave. Here, let me put him on the phone."

"Are you crazy?" I heard her ask him. "After all we've done for you!"

"But Mom, they're trying to push me into a long-term program, and I've done my time here," he said. "It's all about the money. I have a ride to Orlando and need to get back to work."

"You can't stay here," she reminded him. "Where are you going to stay, have you thought about that?"

"Mom, I've gotta go," he said, hanging up. Within a couple hours, he was back in Orlando.

Tommy exited the recovery center with a new girl he'd met there and caught a ride back with her mother, and was now flopping at the mother's house. From the second he had woken up in the hospital several days earlier, and throughout his latest halfhearted recovery attempt, only one thing remained on Tommy's mind: how not to lose his restaurant job.

Despite reassuring him that I had been in regular contact with his manager via text, and that they would welcome him back once he was ready, Tommy loved the job and obsessed about getting back as soon as possible. It led him to pull out all his monitoring wires at the hospital, get dressed, and try to walk out before security guards stopped him. It made him decide to walk out of another recovery center to get back to work after just a few days. But he had a dilemma: no transportation. I'd recovered his scooter in the parking space where he'd left it the night he blacked out. It had been untouched, his valuable bomber jacket lying across the seat. Remarkably, nothing was stolen during the twenty-four hours it sat there. We had parked the scooter in our garage while considering whether to sell it.

My phone soon rang.

"Dad, I need my money," Tommy said.

"How are you going to get back up to the recovery center to get your phone and wallet?" I asked.

"Her mom said she'll give us a ride tomorrow."

Completely disgusted with this misguided change in plans, Mary and I deepened in our resolve not to have him in the house and changed our alarm codes again. I met him at a McDonald's parking lot the next day to give him the cash he'd earned from his job that I'd stashed for safekeeping. *That's it*, I thought like far too many times before. *I probably won't see him again for a long time, if ever.*

Less than two days later Tommy called me, clearly paranoid and terrified. He was hiding in the bushes of a stranger's home, whom he'd somehow convinced to let him use his phone.

"Please come get me as soon as you can," he whispered. "I have to get out of here now."

"Whoa, slow down, I don't even know where you are," I said. "What's happening?"

"It's Six Pack, he's back," he said. "He wants to kill me. Please hurry!"

After jumping in the truck for the thirty-minute drive to his location, I called Tommy back. He proceeded to babble incoherently about Six Pack, a ruthless drug dealer who, according to local news reports, had previously fled to the Dominican Republic to evade capture after killing two people in Orlando. The night before, Tommy had run across the man in a seedy, drug-ridden neighborhood where he had gone with a girl he'd met at the recovery center at which he'd lasted only a week.

The previous day Tommy's new friend convinced her uncle to drive the pair downtown so Tommy could sit down with his restaurant manager to negotiate a return to work. They never made it. The uncle sped down the interstate and while weaving through traffic clipped another car, sending his vehicle careening across three lanes of traffic and causing a four-car wreck. His niece, riding shotgun, suffered a broken nose and cuts from the airbag. The uncle's hand smashed through the windshield, breaking and badly cutting it. Tommy, riding behind the passenger seat and not wearing a seatbelt, was thrown into the seat back and door. He got lucky, suffering mostly from bruised knees and arms. The dark cloud had returned.

That night, frustrated over the accident and hurting from their injuries, Tommy and his friend decided to use Oxys to ease their pain. They climbed in her mother's car and drove off. The neighborhood she drove into made the hair on Tommy's neck stand up, he later told me. It was a territory known to be controlled by the dreaded drug dealer Six Pack, an area Tommy had sworn never to set foot in again. Things got worse.

The woman asked Tommy to wait in the car for her at a convenience store. Tommy was shocked to see her get into another car with a middle-aged man and drive off. It turned out she was turning tricks for drug money, something he says he didn't see coming. Since they'd met in a drug treatment facility just a few days earlier, it's doubtful he knew anything about her. Bored and anxious while awaiting her return, Tommy went into the store to get a bottle of water and some candy. To his horror he heard a familiar voice as the little bells on the store's door announced some new customers entering. It was Six Pack and a couple members of his posse. Tommy ducked down in the aisle and managed to sneak out of the store without Six Pack spotting him. Now terrified but with nothing left to do but wait, he stayed slumped down in the car until the girl returned.

By the next morning Tommy had become convinced that the murderous drug thug he owed money to was also the girl's pimp. He said she had been acting strangely, and he was convinced she'd ratted him out to Six Pack. He was certain that the ruthless dealer was coming to make him pay for his debt. He had left through a back window of the girl's house and was hiding in the bushes outside a nearby home.

On the one hand, there were legitimate reasons to fear Six Pack. Before fleeing the country, Six Pack was the primary suspect in the murder of two young men over a handgun deal gone bad. Both had been shot execution style and their bodies had been set on fire and dumped along a popular bike trail not far from where Tommy was living. The boys' charred bodies were found early the next morning by joggers, and news coverage was extensive. Tommy knew both the victims and the prime suspect in this horrific crime. On the other hand, a person under the haze of heroin is hardly rational and is prone to paranoia and delusion.

I got another call from Tommy from an unknown number.

"Dad, are you almost here?" he whispered.

"What's going on?" I asked.

"Six Pack came looking for me just now. I saw his truck go by the house, slow down, then back up and stop right in front before leaving. I ran out the back and through the yards to escape and rang the doorbell of a nice man who let me use his phone to call you."

He gave me the address.

"I'll be there as soon as I can," I said.

With my adrenaline rising, my phone rang again a few minutes later.

"Is this Tommy's father?" the voice on the other end asked.

"Yes, why?" I asked.

"I'm an officer with the sheriff's department," he said.

My heart sank as I immediately thought Tommy may have been killed.

"I'm here with your son," he said. "He says you're on the way to pick him up. Is this true?"

"Yes, I'll be there in ten minutes," I said, relieved but tense about a potential confrontation with a dangerous drug dealer who might still be lurking about.

After a few minutes during which the deputy explained the situation, I asked him a question.

"Can I ask you something?"

"Sure," he replied.

"Give me your gut feeling," I asked him. "If you were to guess, do you think this drug dealer is really after my son or do you think he's being paranoid and delusional?"

"My guess would be the latter," he said.

"Thank you, officer, I'm almost there."

I pulled up to the house where the owner had let Tommy use his phone, and there were two sheriff deputies, each in their own car, waiting for me. They asked me to follow them and Tommy hopped in my car, looking and acting like someone who had just seen a ghost.

All Tommy's belongings from the recovery center, including a large duffel bag of clothes, a good watch, and his cell phone, were now locked in the new friend's mother's house. Following an argument in which he accused the girl of setting him up, she had left the house and locked up. He'd earlier unlatched a back bathroom window on purpose. The deputy said that under the law he had the right to retrieve his possessions, provided there was a way to get into the house without breaking anything or kicking in a door. With his slender frame, Tommy had no problem slithering through the window and within a couple minutes, he opened the front door to let the deputy inside. Within fifteen minutes, we'd gathered up all of Tommy's things, locked up, and left.

"So here we are again," I said to Tommy calmly. "Help me understand how all this happened. I need details."

Since he'd used drugs less than twenty-four hours earlier, he was still stuck in the "stupid zone," meaning that his logic was circular, his thoughts were all over the board, and his demeanor was jumpy and nervous. Whether or not he'd really seen Six Pack the night before or that morning was irrelevant. We had to find somewhere for him to go.

Moving home was out of the question, I reminded him, giving him the choice between dropping him at a free city recovery program shelter or somewhere on the street. He was terrified to go to a free city shelter, still certain that Six Pack was after him and would be alerted. He also pointed out that most people in such programs were court ordered and were finding ways to use drugs while inside.

"What about Grandma?" he asked. "She and I have been talking, and she says she'll have a room for me in her new house."

"Tommy, she's getting old, gets stressed very easily, and does not need to worry about someone else," I said. "I think it is a bad idea and completely unfair to her."

Mary's reaction to the idea earlier in the day had set her off. "No way, are you crazy!!" she shouted at me over the phone before I hung up on her screaming at me. Not particularly helpful.

"But I've got nowhere else to go," Tommy said. "If I go to one of the detox facilities downtown someone will recognize me and let Six Pack know where I am. He'll kill me! The people in Umatilla are in it for the money, and besides, there's nothing more I'm going to learn at this point."

By the end of our Denny's lunch, his idea of living with his grandmother didn't seem as crazy. By now I had reached the point of just dropping him off at a street corner if that's what he decided he wanted, though I hated the option. My patience for the madness of the past several years had completely run out. As much as we loved our son, there was nothing left we could do to help him if he wouldn't help himself. I no longer harbored the illusion that we could change things for him or keep him afloat. I was at peace that we had done all we could possibly do, and then some. The only certainty was our resolve that we would no longer subject our daughter and ourselves to his self-destructive behavior.

His grandmother Dona had experience dealing with addicts, having worked for many years in social services and having counseled prison inmates, many of them substance abusers, as well as prisoners who had completed their sentences and were attempting to reenter society. Unfortunately, her huge heart made her easy to manipulate, and many years earlier my wife had found out she was going beyond counseling former inmates to sending some of them money to help them regain their footing in the world. Despite such noble intentions and certain street smarts gained growing up in the Bronx, Dona tended to be easily conned. Mary had become furious to learn that while her mother cried poverty to her, she was secretly sending money to ex-cons.

Dona's love for her grandchildren clouded her judgment when it came to Tommy, who seemed to have a special place in her heart. It wasn't as if she hadn't been burned by his manipulative behavior before, such as when he talked her into "lending" him $1,000 to buy his first scooter, the one that landed him in the hospital when he foolishly decided to drive it down a busy highway on a Saturday night. Or the time she had collaborated with our oldest son to bail Tommy out of jail against the wishes of his parents. Or the time he and girlfriend Sarah had stolen and pawned her antique silver to buy drugs.

Despite all this, Dona was ready to take him in. She even drove to Orlando to collect him and what little remained of his possessions.

20

DEATH AND DISCOVERY

Tommy and I paddled our kayaks into the saltwater cove where the manatees were known to gather. There were at least eight of the sea cows splashing in the shallows, breaching partly out of the water. They seemed to be engaged in a game, rolling across and around each other. As we paddled closer, they swam toward us in curiosity, perhaps hoping we'd have something to feed them. They were much larger than we'd realized, and they bumped our kayaks as they swam right under us, rolling onto their backs to look up at us through docile eyes. A couple of them pushed their large snouts out of the water just inches from the kayaks, snorting water out as they got a closer look at the strangers now in their midst.

It was just a few weeks after the Six Pack encounter, and he looked relaxed and happy during my visit. Tommy had wanted to go fishing, but lacking time, boat, and tackle, we settled on renting kayaks instead. It was an idyllic morning with blue skies and big, white fluffy clouds. Best of all, we had the lagoon to ourselves with the exception of the marine mammals, sea birds, and fish who lived here.

I stopped to pull my phone from the plastic bag protecting it, wanting to capture the moment with a picture of my son. Living near the beach with his grandmother seemed to have rejuvenated him, and he looked healthy. Just as I positioned my iPhone to snap the picture, a bottlenose dolphin surfaced just a few feet from Tommy's kayak, and I was able to capture both in the frame. The boy who had always loved dolphins seemed full of joy, at least today.

He worked at local restaurants by night and surfed by day. I helped him attach a special surfboard rack to the side of his scooter, and he became quite a sight riding down the streets and beach, his curly hair flying out from under his backward hat, his tattoos glistening from the salt and sweat. His tan deepened.

"Hobo brown," he said one day with a smirk.

The slower and laid-back pace of the ocean town suited his personality, and he seemed to be in a good place. The stress of his jobs and grandmother would overwhelm him at times, but he mostly spent his days communing with the ocean, playing music with friends, or cooking in restaurants. There was the occasional girl in his life, of course, but even his attitude toward relationships had changed.

"I'm not interested in a relationship at this point," he told me. "I've had enough of that. I want to figure out where I'm going first."

He told his brothers that he never planned to get married or have kids and that he saw himself playing the future role of crazy and fun Uncle Tommy to their kids. Most of all, he loved the peaceful beauty of the beach and ocean, discovering the spiritual connection he had sought but never found. Paddling and surfing for hours, meditating as the sun rose over the water, and quietly observing birds and marine life, he had finally found peace.

For nearly a year, things seemed to finally be clicking for Tommy. He had new friends, was making money, and best of all, was surfing and meditating on a daily basis. It seemed that finally he might find his path forward.

All this changed with a call he received on a fateful Friday afternoon. Sarah, the girlfriend he had once loved so deeply and shared so much with, had died from an opioid overdose.

The news devastated Tommy. He left work early and proceeded to flood his Facebook page with picture after picture of the two of them. When our eldest son, Paul, called Mary to alert her, we immediately knew that he'd become depressed, and we hoped that his circle of friends would provide the support he needed. Mary's brief conversation with Tommy did nothing to ease our worries.

"He's really down," she said. "This is crushing to him."

"I know, but he has a great group of friends and has to learn how to get through the ups and downs of life," I said. "There's nothing we can do unless he wants us to go there or he wants to come here."

"No, he says he's fine and doesn't want us to come," she said. "He's with his friends, and they are comforting him."

"I'll go see him tomorrow," I promised her, then called him myself.

"I'm so sorry, son, I know how hard this has to be."

"She's gone, Dad, it's my fault."

"No, son, it's not your fault; you haven't even seen her in months."

"You don't understand. She has been trying to contact me for weeks, and I blocked her calls and messages," he said between sobs.

"You had to cut off contact to stay clean and rebuild your life."

"I know, but it's not fair. She was the love of my life."

"Can I come over now or tomorrow?" I asked.

"No, I'm okay. My friends are here, and I've got to work tomorrow."

"What about Sunday?"

"That works."

"I'll come over that morning and call you on the way."

"Okay."

"Are you sure you're okay?"

"Yes, I'm okay, just really sad."

"I understand. Stay strong, son, you've worked too hard to give up. This is one of those horrible things that life throws at you, and I know you are in a different place now and can overcome it. I love you."

"I love you too, Dad."

I later learned that Tommy spent a long, tearful evening with friends and on Saturday called in sick and pawned his first item to get enough money to buy drugs. When I arrived on Sunday to walk with him through a natural area of the beach, he seemed fine and appeared to be rebounding from the devastating news.

He blamed himself for first introducing Sarah to Oxys years earlier, for abandoning her in his efforts to preserve his own life, and then for turning his back on her toward the end. They had been completely codependent, unable to separate from each other even when both knew they should.

It was all too much for him, and he convinced himself and us that the stress of living under his grandmother's roof was only adding to his problems.

Desperately wrapped up in his struggle again after nearly one year clean, we reluctantly agreed to help him move out and rent a room from a friend. We had no idea he had resumed using. We also didn't realize that the friend he was moving in with also was likely using, was married with a young child, and had his mother living there as well. On the day we helped him load his bed, dresser, and clothes into my friend's borrowed trailer, we nearly gasped when we laid eyes on the decrepit house he was about to move into. Only slightly better than a clapboard shack, the house was one of several old and poorly maintained homes along the rails, presumably built originally to house railroad workers. As we navigated the trailer to the best spot to unload the furniture, a shirtless old man sat on a dilapidated porch across the narrow street, eyeing us suspiciously while chain-smoking cigarettes. A cute young boy with curly red hair and wearing just pajama bottoms came running out of the house into which Tommy was moving to greet us.

"Hi, Tommy, who are they?" he asked.

During introductions I couldn't help but notice horrific burn scars across the boy's chest. We later learned that he was being homeschooled by his mother, did not attend the public elementary school just two blocks away, and was recovering from lice.

Inside the house was a disaster, full of cats, kittens, and a couple of dogs. The place was filthy and completely cluttered, which Tommy blamed on the fact that his friend and family had just moved in and hadn't yet had enough time to unpack.

Mary and I sensed immediately that drug use had to be a big part of the puzzle, having by now observed similar unmitigated messes in other places we'd visited or retrieved Tommy. We wished him luck and drove home, certain that this would be a very short-term arrangement. It was. Tommy, who had begun using again on the day after Sarah's death, soon got into a fight with his friend's mother over a late rent payment and was asked to leave. While attempting to network at a business conference in Scottsdale, my phone rang over and over. It was Tommy.

"Dad, can you rent me a U-Haul? They threw all my stuff out on the porch in garbage bags, and I have to get everything out of there before it rains."

"Tommy, I'm out of town and am not going to be able to do this for a couple hours, will that work? What about Grandma?"

"She won't help me."

"Give me a little time, and I'll see what I can do."

Within hours, a U-Haul truck was secured via my credit card, and Tommy and a friend got his stuff out of the rotting house. Since his grandmother refused to let him store his furniture in her garage, he spent the next twenty-four hours aimlessly driving around trying to figure out what to do, racking up one hundred miles on the rented truck. The next day he took the furniture to a friend's shed and returned to his grandma's house to resume residence on her sofa bed. His brief shot at independence over, Tommy fell further into depression.

Within days I received a frantic call from Dona.

"I'm really worried about Tommy, he's not himself and I'm afraid. He's irritable and slept twenty straight hours on my couch."

211

"Who are you talking to?" I heard Tommy ask in the background.

"I'm talking to your father," she shouted. "Now he's asking me to loan him ten dollars because his car is out of gas."

"That's not true; stop exaggerating, Grandma," I heard him yell in anger.

"Look, I can't deal with this. Can you talk to him?"

"Put him on the phone," I said.

"I can't do this anymore," Tommy said, crying, his voice barely audible.

"You relapsed, right?"

"Yes."

"Did you try to overdose?"

"Yes."

"Tommy, do you realize that dying is the worst thing you could ever do to your family?" I asked, fighting back tears. "We love you so much, and you've been doing so well."

"I just couldn't see any other way out," he said, still crying. "I dug the hole so deep this time that I just didn't know how to get out."

From the time Sarah died three weeks earlier, Tommy had lost it all. He'd returned to drugs, lost his job, lost his place to live, sold his most prized belongings—his guitar and surfboard—and was ready to die.

"I've got to think at this point that it's not only the drugs but that there are other issues making you feel so depressed that might be treatable," I said, grasping for anything that might convince him to stay at his grandmother's house and not walk out the door as he was threatening to do. "Do you think that there might be more to this than just the drugs?"

"I don't know, Dad, I think maybe."

"Will you wait for me? I can be there in an hour."

"I don't know; you guys have done so much for me. I don't deserve to live. I'm a failure. You would be much better off without me."

"Tommy, that's not true! We love you and will never give up on you. Please, don't give up on yourself. We can get through this. Okay?"

"I don't know, just let me go!"

"Tommy!" I said in as stern a voice as possible without losing a compassionate tone. "I'll be there in an hour, and we can talk about this in person. Okay?"

After a slight pause he answered. "Okay."

"Hang tight, try to eat something. I'll be there as fast as possible. We love you!"

A little over an hour later, Tommy and I were in my truck and heading back to Orlando to a new treatment center that Mary had found. This one combined a full psychological assessment with the drug recovery program, and seemed to take a more clinical approach than any recovery and rehab centers we'd encountered. Still panning for a golden nugget that might save our son, we reasoned that maybe his inability to stay clean was rooted in psychiatric imbalance, not just physical dependency.

By the time Tommy's relapses had hit double digits, I'd concluded that brain chemistry and underlying mental imbalances had to be major ingredients in the complex stew that leads to addiction. Why do some in the same family with similar genetic predispositions toward substance abuse become addicts while others don't? Why are some addicts able to overcome and have clean, productive lives while others can't? How can some folks simply stop smoking, drinking, or drugging cold turkey and never touch their crutch again without any programs, meetings, or outside help? Brain chemistry is a powerful piece of the mix. Everyone is different, and in considering the struggles faced by my son, brother, and late father—coupled with the countless stories I've digested about other addicts over the past several years— I'm convinced that our individual wiring is a leading factor in addiction to drugs, food, sex, or any excess. The brain is the last frontier for modern medicine, yet we're essentially in the Stone Age when it comes to truly understanding it.

In Tommy's case, psychological testing had been conducted a year or two earlier, diagnosing him with social anxiety disorder and mild depression. It was impossible to decipher whether these conditions were preexistent or related to the rewiring of brain circuits that five years of hard drug use had caused. The dilemma is even greater when considering potential treatment using medicine. How can you prescribe pills to a pill abuser? What if we were just giving him something more to abuse or something that would kill him by interacting with the Oxys he was injecting?

The chemical-imbalance issue combined with his drug abuse thrust Tommy into no-man's-land when it came to finding a doctor to help us sort things out. Most psychiatrists refuse to even see a patient with a history of drug dependency, not to mention that getting an appointment for a new patient can often take months. The demand far outstrips the supply of doctors, something that was exasperated by repercussions from the pill-mill problem and Big Pharma's prowess at peddling pills for every ailment imaginable.

The long-term vexing problem of how and whether to treat Tommy's social anxiety and depression had now resurfaced.

On our drive back to Orlando, he agreed that it might be time to try medicine, although because he was still coming down off opiates, there wasn't much coherent thought coming out of him that day. Instead of traveling to Barry's campus for a planned weekend visit, I found myself sitting in the waiting room of another facility discovered in our latest foraging for a panacea.

Within the first thirty minutes of our arrival, I sensed this was a mistake. On the ten or so previous occasions when I'd checked Tommy into a detox facility, the process was the same—private interview with the patient, payment terms arranged, and then the patient taken to a bed inside fifteen to twenty minutes maximum. This time we found ourselves still waiting to see someone after three hours! The center apparently had no clue how to deal with individuals coming down from heroin or pills.

The first sign that we should have left shortly after arrival was the thirty-something woman who appeared more like fifty who was pacing the room and swearing at any staff person who came in or out of the locked doors.

"How much longer?" she cackled. "I've been here for two hours!"

Clearly also coming down and, like my son, beginning to experience nausea, cramps, and extreme irritability, the woman was fit to be tied. Except for stepping outside a couple times to bum and smoke a cigarette, she became louder and more belligerent as the clock kept ticking. Eventually, she was kicking furniture around, cussing, and threatening to leave. The tension she added to the waiting room impacted Tommy almost immediately, especially given his condition and acute sensitivity to the environment and those around him.

"Dad, this is BS, let's just leave," he said several times.

"No, son, we have to stick it out," I insisted.

I went back to the check-in window several times to complain and explain that you can't expect someone coming off opiates to sit in a waiting room for hours. I demanded to speak to a doctor or anyone in charge. The college student working the front desk was kind and tried to get someone to come up front, but no one did. Adding further insult to our experience, a pair of uniformed first responders entered escorting a teenage boy who was absorbed with a game on his cell phone. Within five minutes, a nurse came out to take him inside, and the two men left. *So if I had him arrested or brought in by ambulance, he would be seen right away?* I thought, more frustrated than angry. After what seemed like an eternity, at least they took the other woman back, and we didn't have to listen to her rants anymore.

But before long a worse agitator entered the picture, a hard-looking man that sat two seats down from us. I heard him offer Tommy the worst possible information, given that by now Tommy was itching constantly, sweating, and beginning to suffer from cramps.

"If you haven't been here before, it's Friday, so the doctors have left for the weekend," he said. "They won't be giving you any real meds for the withdrawals."

Hearing this, Tommy predictably decided we must leave and said that if I didn't take him out, he'd walk out and find his own ride.

Again I marched up to the window and asked to speak with a supervisor, and again no one came out. I convinced Tommy to give it a little longer.

Nearly three hours from the time we arrived, a very young attendant, likely an intern or medical student and moving the speed of a snail, shuffled over to let us know we could not have the evaluation-for-admittance interview until Tommy filled out about thirty pages of medical history, questionnaires, and related paperwork.

I couldn't help myself. "Are you kidding me; we've been sitting here three hours and now you give us all this paperwork that we could have completed long ago? Does anyone here have the first clue about opioid withdrawal?"

The woman did not apologize; she simply stared vacantly at me, the type of "I don't give a damn" stare that Tommy had when on opioids, a look that drives me nuts. Then she slowly plodded away and disappeared, the buzz and slam of the heavy security door sounding her exit. Despite his protests, I insisted he complete the reams of paperwork, and Tommy angrily scribbled on the pages, practically breaking the point of the pen as he slammed it against each new page on the clipboard.

About twenty minutes later, the same woman returned and decided she could not accept some of the pages left blank or containing illegible scribbles.

"All questionnaires and paperwork must be filled out completely before you can be screened," she said.

I tried to hand her the papers and explained the torture they were putting an addict through who was in severe pain from withdrawal, and she again gave me the blank stare as if to say, "I couldn't care less about your son or you" before slinking away.

About forty-five minutes later, having wasted nearly four hours in that useless place without seeing a doctor, I agreed with Tommy that enough was enough and we left. I peeled out of the parking lot and Tommy said, "Dad, calm down, you're going to kill us driving like that."

How ironic, I thought.

For the second time we would detox our son in the comfort of the home he grew up in. Hours earlier I'd insisted that Mary drive the two hours north to be with Barry for the weekend as planned, as much for his sake as my own. The communication channels Tommy and I had opened nearly a year earlier had remained open except for the three-week period between Sarah's death and now. Having just the two of us home during his first day of detox seemed like a blessing.

"Son, what do you need?" I asked as we drove home. "You've been through this enough times now that you know what will get you through."

"I need cigarettes," he said. "Also, some Gatorade to help me stay hydrated."

"Anything else?"

"Well, there is one more thing, but I'm afraid you'll get mad."

"What?"

"A little bit of weed. It's the only way my mind will shut down long enough to help me sleep."

"What about withdrawal medicine, like they give you in detox centers?"

"That would be good, but it's not essential."

With that I swung by a convenience store to pick up cigarettes and Gatorade. I called Mary to let her know I would not be coming and to fill her in. A neighbor friend of Tommy's swung by and left a pipe and small amount of marijuana behind a chair on our porch. Fortunately, my daughter Jessie was out with a friend, and we arrived to a dark and quiet house.

I set Tommy up on a couch in our rec room where he would have a television and easy access to an outside area where he could smoke as needed. I got him a vomit bucket, pillow, and blanket. As he lay down, our dog, Mo, immediately jumped up on the couch and curled up next to him. If any combination of our six family members is together with Tommy present, Mo will always be found next to him. If left outside Tommy's door, he will cry to be let into his room and refuse to leave his side in the morning. It's as if the small dog senses the innate kindness in Tommy's soul. They are inseparable, and Tommy regularly tries to convince his mother to let him take Mo to live with him, but she refuses.

When Jessie arrived home late after seeing a movie, I gave her an honest account of the situation. At first she reacted in anger.

"Why, Dad? What the heck!" she said. "Why is he here? He'll only steal from us or hurt us again!"

"Jessie, calm down, you have to understand."

"Understand what?" she replied, becoming sarcastic. "Help me understand."

I explained that the only hope he had was the love and support of his family and that no matter what he was our family, and we could not turn our backs on him. She began to cry, then ran toward the room where Tommy was resting.

"Jessie, no," I called. "You'll wake him."

There was no stopping her, and as I turned the corner I saw her sitting on the couch embraced in a hug with her favorite brother.

"I love you, Tommy," she said between sobs. "Don't die!"

She then headed to her room and collapsed on her bed, still crying. I tried to reason with her, distraught over her continued sobbing.

"C'mon, Jessie, take it easy."

"Shut up, Dad, leave me alone!"

Irritated, I foolishly responded with an ill-timed teaching moment. It had been a long day.

"This isn't about you, Jessie, it's about Tommy," I said. "Don't go putting something up on social media or telling all your friends. It will not help him to get a bunch of phone calls or have some of his drug friends find out he's back in Orlando."

"Oh, so you want me to cover it up," she snapped. "Don't worry, I won't *embarrass* the family."

"That's not my point."

"Then what is your point, Dad, that I'm too immature or stupid to not blab?"

"Jessie, why are you making this a fight between us?"

"Look in the mirror."

"That's not fair. This is tough on all of us. All I'm asking is that you respect his privacy. He needs our love and understanding most of all."

"I understand. I'm sorry."

Both of us calmed down. I hugged her, told her I loved her, and urged her to try to get some sleep. She had an important standardized ACT test early the next morning.

I walked to the other end of the house to check on Tommy. He was lying on the couch, Mo curled up next to his chest, and resting peacefully. For the first time since I'd picked him up that day, his mind seemed calm. His demeanor was totally opposite from the nasty, on-edge temperament I'd experienced during hours in the waiting room. It struck me how much better this arrangement was than further isolating him by pushing him into a hospital with strangers for a week. That would have been another short-term way to kick the can down the road and pay $5,000 for the privilege!

About seven years after the stressful rescue of our son from an abandoned building, I finally understood that there was no combination of meetings, medicines, doctors, therapists, or programs that were ever going to save our son. Only unconditional love and acceptance from his family would have a chance of succeeding. A major bridge had been crossed in my mind. Now I had to figure out how to help Mary and my kids see the light.

21

COLLECT MEMORIES, NOT STUFF

When we arrived at the small house in a gritty section of the Gulf Coast city, we could see Tommy's hooded jacket draped over the railing on the front porch. There was only one problem. A menacing pit bull terrier patrolled the chain link fence in the front yard.

As the dog barked and snarled at us, a burly tattooed neighbor came walking across the street with a warning. "I wouldn't go in there. She's mean."

Tommy agreed, not knowing the dog well enough and not willing to fetch his jacket with her loose in the yard. Stubbornly, I decided to get the jacket myself, just one more in a long series of hotheaded decisions made in the relentless madness of my son's addiction. I sized up the dog, made myself as tall and menacing as possible, opened the fence gate, and stepped into the yard. The dog took a couple steps toward me barking and showing her teeth.

"Get back," I yelled, advancing slowly toward the porch. I sensed a small measure of fear in the dog's eyes, and as I continued moving slowly toward the porch, she backed up rather than charge me. After what seemed to be a lot longer than it really was, I was able to grab the jacket and began to slowly back away, now trying to calm the agitated dog by saying, "Good girl, good girl."

As I backed out of the yard and closed the gate, the charge finally came. The dog launched herself against the closed gate barking and snapping her jaws wildly. But we were safely on the outside and soon on our way.

In retrospect, one of the stupidest things Mary and I stressed over each time one of our son's recovery attempts failed was his stuff. Many times we bought him new clothes to replace what he'd lost, but each time we channeled some of our frustration and anger into usually futile attempts to recover his belongings, often resulting in heated confrontations with halfway house or pawnshop owners.

While recovery centers generally did a decent job of safeguarding what few things he was allowed to bring, halfway houses were a different story; they were dens of thieves. Day after day unknown housemates would steal clothes, cheap electronic devices, and anything else they could find. Our son's frustration with this situation would grow with each stolen item. On this particular day, I'd risked being bitten by a protective dog to retrieve a hoodie that Mary insisted we must recover. I had hounded Tommy, and it had taken him several attempts to reach the friend at whose house he'd left it. The friend, naturally, wasn't home.

Both Mary and I grew up in working middle-class households shattered by divorce, and even though my parents grew up during the Great Depression and Mary's mother was born at the end of it, their mindsets were the same: everything had more than one use, and nothing was ever to be thrown away. Going out to a restaurant, a staple in our children's lives, was a rare luxury for Mary and me in our childhoods. Instead of going to Hampton Inns with free breakfasts, Mary recalls her childhood vacations as camping and sleeping in tents. I can remember having to wear the same clothes for a long time, even when slacks became "high-waders" as I grew taller. We didn't feel poor, but we both were acutely aware of how hard our parents worked for very little money. We were taught to appreciate and hang on to what we had worked hard to earn.

Tommy's mindset couldn't be more opposite. The ease with which he simply let material items drift away without a care went far beyond his trading them for drug money. Whether he lost an article of clothing or an automobile, his attitude was the same.

"That's the problem with the world, Dad," he told me. "It used to be we just used what we needed, and people weren't as caught up with material things. It's too bad we can't get back to that and share what we have with those who are in need."

His losses infuriated us; he simply never cared.

I was mulling this over while pulling into the airport to pick up my friend Mike who had flown in from Connecticut for the outdoor music festival our family and friends have been attending for several years in northern Florida.

"Mike, I have some bad news. I've got a little bit of a curveball I need to deal with today."

"Tommy?" he asked.

"How'd you know?"

"I figured. I saw something on Paul's Facebook."

"Listen, today is a search and rescue mission," I explained. "I've got to go to the beach with Tommy to buy back his stuff from pawnshops. He's very depressed. He had stayed clean nearly a year this time. You can hang out at the house or come with us, whatever you want to do."

"I'm in!"

"Okay, Sgt. Slaughter, a search and rescue mission it is!"

By the time we were halfway to the beach, a dejected Tommy in the backseat, I could see through the rearview mirror that he was beginning to relax. He even cracked a brief smile at one of Mike's crazy comments. Big Mike was just the tonic our son needed to lighten the painful process of repurchasing the most valuable items he had pawned during his relapse after Sarah's death. Mike's smile and loud laugh were larger than life, like Jackie Gleason in *The Honeymooners* when he thought one of his get-rich schemes was working. Mike's positive energy is contagious, and it was the perfect icebreaker on what was a very tough day.

By the time we reached the small surfer village on the Atlantic Ocean, Tommy was interacting with us. We were talking music, turning each other on to various bands and songs. The pawnshop where his scooter now resided was closed, meaning we'd have to repeat the journey the following day. At the second pawnshop we encountered a young man and woman in filthy clothing, their rail-thin bodies obviously ravaged from drug use.

225

"Hi, Tommy," they said as we walked in, exchanging hugs with him.

Catching the stern glare I didn't try hard to hide, they completed their transaction and left.

"See you around, Tommy," the girl said.

Mike and I checked out the antique guns, vinyl record albums, guitars, and other oddities while Tommy waited in line. The place was as depressing as a Reno casino on a Tuesday night, with down-on-their-luck folks staring vacantly at the slot machines gobbling up their rent money. The shop was a far cry from TV's *Pawn Stars*; you could almost feel the stories of woe behind the worn power tools, décor items, and glassware throughout the shop.

"How much?" I asked Tommy, trying to help him at least preserve his dignity by handing over the money to regain his items.

His prized electric bass guitar and banjo now safely tucked in my truck, we headed to lunch, at which Mike again lightened Tommy's mood with typical hilarity. We returned the following day to collect the motor scooter, and I noticed that though Tommy was still fragile, he was slowly climbing back.

22

THE PATH
TO ACCEPTANCE

The streets of the eastern Pennsylvania village seemed straight out of a postapocalyptic horror movie, complete with the occasional zombie shuffling slowly down a sidewalk or alley. Many once-thriving storefronts were boarded up with graffiti-covered plywood. The handful of stores, bars, and restaurants that survived were plastered with discount or specials stickers, indicating their continuing fight to survive. Most of the few cars that passed by were old and rusted out, their driving days dwindling.

The town, once spotless and idyllic, nearly Norman Rockwell–esque the time we'd visited twenty years earlier, had not been devastated by bombs, floods, or fires. This disaster was man-made, the result of economic depression and drugs, including the heroin and black market pill epidemic that continues to destroy similar towns across America. The life forms ambling through the streets were shells of the humans they had been before heroin, meth, and other poisons of escape ravaged their bodies.

Mary and I were here on a whim to join several friends for a fun weekend and to experience what a NASCAR race was all about in the rural North. It wasn't until a rainy day canceled our outdoor plans that we went downtown in search of a restaurant or bar and found ourselves in this sad, beaten-down place. We were stunned that the pretty village with bright American flags and sparkling lampposts had become so dilapidated. We certainly knew the terrible impact the offshoring of jobs and the opioid and meth epidemics had on much of rural America, including my own hometown. Across the Delaware River in northwest New Jersey, the general area where Tommy had twice lived with my brother and mother, I'd driven through similar towns. This seemed worse. Our son's struggles had removed all blinders and filters, and my eyes were now fully opened, seeing everything.

Like the bartender from the motel in which we were staying slipping out the side door to complete a drug transaction in the parking lot. And the piercing, sketchy stares from clearly strung-out parents who were living in parts of the motel with their kids, apparently part of a section 8 housing arrangement. And the forty-something covered with track marks stumbling up the street, underwear showing, shirt fully unbuttoned, legs bloody at eleven in the morning. By now I had seen these things all too often. It was definitely not what we had in mind when we agreed to join our friends for a spur-of-the-moment race weekend.

At last the problem was receiving mainstream attention. The opioid epidemic that began with Purdue's OxyContin rollout and market dominance was virtually unchecked for the first decade. This was more than enough time for legalized drug pushers to establish distribution networks into states in the South, Appalachia, and ultimately across the nation. Particularly in the northeastern and New England states, the problem was compounded by easy access to heroin itself, with the drug flowing through seaports from Maryland to Maine. Tommy had managed to live near the center of both growing epidemics thanks to his two stints in heroin-flooded New Jersey.

In 2007, Purdue was finally held accountable with its admission that it had provided misleading information while building its OxyContin empire. It absorbed the $600 million in fines rather easily given the profits it continued to rake in from its multibillion dollar cash cow.

Sadly, it took nearly another decade before elected officials and regulators, whose silence had been bought for many years by the powerful Big Pharma lobby, decided they could no longer afford to ignore the issue. President Obama proposed $1.1 billion in budget spending dedicated to combating the opioid and heroin epidemic in 2016. In various states several of the same politicians who for years gladly accepted Big Pharma contributions suddenly woke up, staging press conferences to announce bold new programs. Most of these election-year initiatives did little to address the root causes of opiate addiction but instead were Band-Aid approaches, such as arming police, fire, and emergency medical personnel with naloxone, a drug that can save lives by reversing the effects of an overdose. Making the drug available to men and women on the front lines of the opiate epidemic—first responders who are far more expert in the subject than the talking heads often seen pontificating about it in the media—was a positive step that has already saved many lives. But it is a Band-Aid solution that treats only the symptoms, not the cause.

As was the case in Florida with the initial pill-mill shutdown, the moves to cut off the opioid spigot were staged for maximum publicity, with TV news outlets gladly obliging. But there remains no concerted strategy for what comes next. Typical of our bloated bureaucracies in Washington, DC, and state capitols, there seems to be a complete lack of coordination or a strategic game plan for tackling a problem that continues to kill so many.

When states began restricting access to prescription pills containing oxycodone, opioid-dependent users like Tommy didn't just stop using; they switched to the original and even more dangerous killer, street heroin. It was cheaper and a major game changer. Heroin and black market copycat versions of Oxys are often laced with powerful, deadly chemicals such as fentanyl to extend supply and profits. With street dealers now in the driver's seat, heroin flooded the market, introducing a broad demographic of prescription-pill addicts to a drug once considered an inner-city scourge. Unlike the factory-precise pills addicts had grown familiar with, the street heroin killing kids today is often cut with enough nasty chemicals that even hardcore users cannot gauge strength levels. As drug dealers' profits soar, the death count rises.

The two regions where Tommy spent his teens and early twenties had the highest heroin death rates, according to a CDC report analyzing 2010–12, the period that included many users switching from harder-to-get and more expensive Oxys to heroin. During this time the heroin overdose death rate more than doubled in the twenty-eight states measured, rising 211 percent in the northeast and 181 percent in the South.[1] Prescription opioid fatalities were less than one-half of a percent lower.

The utter devastation this epidemic brought to families across the nation, as well as entire neighborhoods and small towns such as the one we visited in Pennsylvania, caught the attention of the mainstream media and Hollywood in 2016. Producer Rob Reiner and his son made a movie about his son's struggle with opioids. The overdose death of Prince, reportedly linked to Oxy addiction, has further pushed the subject into the spotlight. Yet the death stats keep climbing. More than ninety Americans die each day from opioid overdose. To put this in perspective, about twelve soldiers per day died during the Vietnam War, and statistically less than two per day lost their lives during the height of fighting in Iraq and Afghanistan. But there has been no public outcry or marching in the streets related to this epidemic. Shrouded by the stigma of inner-city heroin addiction as portrayed in '70s pop culture, addiction still occurs mostly in the shadows, slowly decimating families across the economic and demographic spectrum.

Tommy slept twelve straight hours following our stressful waiting-room debacle and return home. I read a full psychiatric profile that had been conducted on him nearly two years earlier while he dozed. Mary had tried to get me to read it several times before, but I was too raw and couldn't bring myself to do so. Social anxiety disorder combined with mild depression was the official diagnosis, but the report had no real recommendations on how to address it.

We were convinced that a person's mental state is at the root of most substance abuse, but how to tackle this remained the dilemma. We've learned that long-term opioid abuse can rewire brain circuitry, but to some extent isn't that what any prescription drug for psychiatric disorders does? How can you use drugs to treat a condition in a person prone to abuse drugs?

During his freshman year in high school, Tommy had once been on ADD medicine that he claimed helped him stay focused and do better at school. But we soon learned he was abusing pain pills, and we feared having him take any prescription meds that could be abused. Psychiatrists he saw along the way were all about pushing pill solutions, usually after only fifteen-minute consults—that is, if you were lucky to get in to see one at all. They seemed to be experimenting with various pharmaceuticals to find the right combination that worked, yet none ever had time to get to really know Tommy or evaluate underlying causes that might be at work. Eventually he manipulated these doctors to get the types of meds he favored to numb his pain. By this point, Tommy knew as much about various pills as the doctors did, and we sensed he was simply using them to feed his addiction. Our concerns were later justified after he turned eighteen and insisted on visiting unscrupulous doctors at pill mills or new psychiatric offices throughout the region.

To their defense, the medical professionals we interacted with over the past eight years appeared overwhelmed and harried by skyrocketing demand. The opioid epidemic, overall pharmaceutical explosion, and deteriorating societal conditions combined to create a very untenable situation in Florida and elsewhere. If any legitimate psychiatrist found Tommy had been abusing drugs, they immediately dismissed him as a patient, likely for liability concerns, leaving him to choose from the quacks and pill pushers lining their pockets during the pharmaceutical gold rush.

Through a doctor friend, Mary obtained a prescription for a nonaddictive substitute for the Suboxone, methadone, or other withdrawal meds used at most detox facilities. Predictably, Tommy at first threw a fit.

"That won't help," he said. "Just get me some Suboxone."

We were determined not to repeat past mistakes and remained firm in our decision.

"No, Tommy. This will help with the nausea and cramping. It will help get you off the drugs without just making you dependent on something else."

"But I've been taking it since yesterday, and it has done nothing," he whined.

We didn't back down. About a year earlier, we had noticed sluggish and dopey behavior that usually was the precursor to a full relapse. Instead of Oxys or heroin, we found he had been taking far more Suboxone than the doctor advised and was also buying additional supplies from friends. As has often been questioned with methadone, this was a not a substance that helped him overcome addiction; it was a crutch that kept the dependency going in a much more functional way.

After a visit to my therapist David's office, at which he lauded our decision to detox Tommy at home, I laid out a written plan on a piece of graph paper for next steps. I felt we had never really checked the box on finding a medicine that might even out Tommy's anxiety. Despite our past experiences and our concerns about psychiatrists and pharmaceuticals, I felt he should at least try a low dose of something that might help balance his brain chemistry. A low-dose of ADD medicine I've been taking for years has helped, I believe, temper past feelings of depression and mood swings. A college friend who had become so imbalanced through LSD use that his delusions persisted even when sober had found balance through lithium and gone on to become a wealthy and happy family man. Perhaps during the chaos of past years, we'd never truly given Tommy the opportunity to find the right medicine that could help him. On the other hand, I rationalized, because he was actively using Oxys, nothing would have worked anyway.

Mary disagreed. Tommy had become irritable and nasty. She was fed up. Strangely, I was calm and resolved.

"He needs your patience and acceptance," I told her. "I know this is the right thing to do. I've got this."

His detox recipe seemed to be working, and we did our best to help him celebrate his twenty-fourth birthday two days after coming home, sharing our love and acceptance despite nursing the latest wounds to our hearts. We even baked him a birthday cake, which of course he couldn't eat, his body still working hard to overcome the poisons he had put into his system the previous several days. Tommy was thoroughly depressed and defeated. At first, I couldn't tell if it was because he was upset that his latest attempt at death by overdose had not succeeded. Over the next couple of days, however, it became clear through our brief conversations that he wanted to live.

By Sunday, as Tommy's withdrawal symptoms began to subside, we were facing a difficult decision. For the past three years we had taken our sons along with several friends to a music festival held in a beautiful setting along the Suwanee

River in northern Florida. We were scheduled to depart, complete with RV, tents, and gear, just four days from now. A handful of friends were flying in, with Big Mike scheduled to be the first to arrive the following day. At first, Mary, Paul, and Barry were adamant as they weighed in independently. Under no circumstances should Tommy attend.

"What are you going to do about Tommy?" Barry asked on a call. "I don't think he should go."

"We'll have to see how he's doing," Mary had said after we briefly disagreed about the subject and I wouldn't back down. "One day at a time."

"You're crazy!" Paul said. "What are you thinking?"

I found myself in a different place, the transition complete after the wasted hours on Friday in the clueless clinic. I was clear and certain. The worst possible thing we could do for our son at this point was to isolate him, just as the worst thing two days earlier would have been to leave him to detox in a ward full of strangers and interns. I knew he needed me, needed all of us, and that our love and acceptance was the most important thing we could give him to help him pull himself slowly up from the floor. Anything less would trigger the feelings of rejection and worthlessness that had knocked him down so many times before. This time I refused to leave his side, regardless of what anyone else thought.

The following day on the drive to the airport to pick up Mike, I got Paul and Barry on a three-way call to make my position clear. After patiently listening to their concerns, several of which seemed somewhat selfish, I cut in.

"Look, this is not your decision. You're not the parents, we are. I appreciate how much you are trying to help and also how hard you're trying to protect your mom and me.

We both know how much you've been through and that your hearts are in the right place. But Tommy needs us now more than ever. We bought the tickets as a family, and we're going to go as a family. I'm not expecting you guys to do anything special, just treat him like you always do. Just accept him and love him like normal."

"I understand," Paul replied. "We just don't want you to get hurt."

"I get it," Barry said.

"I'm going to be straight with you," I said. "Tommy felt so guilty and low following Sarah's death that he felt like ending it all. He told me that the hole he dug was so deep he didn't see any other way out. There's only one way he can get out, and that's through his family. We're already on the right path, and he's feeling better.

"I know you'll have to see the proof for yourself, but he's in a different place this time. He was clean almost a year before this. This was a major slip, yes, but it also came after the death of someone he loved and spent nearly two years with. I get it. I also know that the last thing he needs is to be shipped off somewhere or babysat while the rest of us go up there. He knows Mike, he knows Jen, and he has you guys and tons of friends. This will be the best thing for him now. It's not like he's going to score H or Oxys at a hippy festival, and if he smokes a little weed, oh well. The most important thing is that he will be with us. Plus, the music will be good for him."

"Understood," Paul said.

"Got it," Barry said.

"I love you both."

"Love you too, Pops," Paul said.

"Me too," Barry said.

During this period it was difficult to keep Mary at bay. While she nurtured and showed him great love and affection, she couldn't seem to keep from asking him useless backward-looking questions about what had happened or premature forward-leaning questions about what would come next. To a lesser extent, I also occasionally found myself wanting to probe him for clues about his relapse.

Living in the present is probably the most difficult thing any person can do, especially in our culture of consumption, materialism, and immediate gratification. Through more than a decade of on-again and off-again therapy, I'd become conscious of a flaw in my psyche, yet was rarely able to practice what I knew would ease my mind—appreciating each day and each moment of life itself. I grew to lament that I'd wasted far too much of my life feeling sorry for myself about the past or worried about the future, when the only thing I really had control over was the present. Too often I was envious of friends who had great relationships with their dads. Other times I'd use the darkness and dysfunction of my childhood as a crutch, an excuse to eat or drink to excess or retreat from meaningful connection with my wife, family, and friends. My father was a loner, and in some ways so am I.

The journey with Tommy helped me understand and finally shed some of these feelings. Like my father, I am a flawed man who, though far more engaged in his sons' lives, wasn't always emotionally present when physically there. Instead of holding my father to some vision of what I thought a good dad should be, I began to see him in a more realistic light, and thankfully forgave him for his shortcomings a few years before his passing. Had I understood this earlier and forgiven him sooner, I may have avoided years of self-doubt and inner unhappiness. Perhaps I would have become a better husband, father, and friend. My father has been gone for more than a decade, and my middle son's journey is far from over. Yet whatever happens I now sleep peacefully knowing I gave all the love in my heart and did the best I could, just as my dad did the best he could for me.

As Tommy helped me discover over time, my own upbringing had far less to do with who I became than I once thought, just as who Tommy has become had much less to do with me than I once blamed myself for. A parent can no more control their postpubescent child than they can control the weather. Sure, you can influence a child's values, faith, and behavior, but once they reach the middle-teen years, the more you try to control instead of counsel, the worse the results will be. Maybe a daughter's rebellion won't occur until her freshman year of college. Under the thumb of a controlling parent, perhaps a son will learn to hide his rebellion from you. But it will come out eventually. Part of a child's evolution into an adult is the transition to making independent decisions as a teenager, including enjoying the results of good decisions and suffering the natural consequences of bad ones. The more you try to control their decisions, leaving teenagers ill-equipped to manage the real world when away at college or at their first jobs, the worse the results usually are.

If you pause to think about it, the same applies to all our relationships, not just those with our children. Ultimately, the only person we can control is the one who greets us in the bathroom mirror each morning. What comes out of our mouth has perhaps the most important impact on the lives of others. Words of acceptance, love, and encouragement are absolutely critical to instilling our kids with self-worth.

Disparaging and hurtful words have the opposite effect. How we choose to react to the actions and moods of others is also within our control. Just because someone else is having a bad morning does not mean that we have to. Why not ignore a negative attitude or, better yet, attempt to thaw an icy stare with a smile? Our culture is harsher and more self-centered than ever before, and our children are surrounded by negativity every day. We can't shield them from an unkind world, but we can make our homes a safe haven—but only if we control our own words and actions.

When a teen or young adult is abusing drugs, the control dilemma is magnified. Only they can choose to help themselves, something it took Mary and me many years to fully recognize. Instead, we repeatedly denied this reality, disrupting our lives with ill-fated rescue attempts and plunging our family into extensive debt by flushing tens of thousands of dollars down the recovery-industry bowl. Our physical and mental health, as well as that of Tommy's siblings, was negatively impacted by our relentless efforts to heal him. We could have saved ourselves immense grief and much money if we'd recognized earlier that we had no more chance of "saving" Tommy than we had of changing the tides and that family love was the key to his survival.

23

BATTLEGROUND MUSINGS

We both scrambled to get our shorts back on, giggling in embarrassment. Skinny-dipping in this pristine lake in the mountains of Arkansas had seemed like a perfect way to cool off and refresh ourselves for the long drive ahead. The late afternoon sun and beautiful foliage reflected off the clear water like a mirror, causing us to slow down, make a U-turn, and head into the state park. We found a spot near the boat launch where we could swim out of sight of the road.

Suddenly, Tommy and I saw what looked like a park ranger pickup truck heading down the road toward the launch ramp, and we realized that not taking the time to dig out our bathing suits from the suitcases inside the roof rack had not been a wise choice. At least he stopped one hundred yards away to give us time to rush out of the lake and get dressed. The anticipated tongue-lashing was brief.

"You're not supposed to be swimming in this area," he said. "You are allowed to swim only in the designated area."

We had seen the signs. But since it was past the summer season and there wasn't a soul around, we had thought there was no harm in taking a dip somewhere more private than the roped-off area in plain view from the road.

"Sorry, there was no one around and we were just taking a quick dip to cool off while passing through," I replied.

"This is a state park, and you are also supposed to pay to use it."

"Again, sorry about this. We'll pay on the way out."

We tucked a five-dollar bill into the honor system park box and headed back up another mountain. We were traveling west, taking nearly all back roads through the most rural areas we could find on the map. Just two days into our cross-country voyage, we were fully enjoying each other's company and appreciating the beauty we were seeing. It struck me on this trip that Tommy was the most like me out of all our children, something I had never seen before. When our children were little, we often drove back and forth between Florida and New York or other points north, a couple times even pulling a waterski boat behind the Suburban. On many of these voyages, when the rest of the family was asleep and therefore unable to protest, I'd snuck onto back roads, leaving the interstate to see what the areas really looked like. I now recognized that Tommy was the only other family member who shared my love of back roads and discovery along the way. The other four favored detouring only for spectacular points of interest; otherwise they preferred to get to the final destination as fast as possible.

"Another one of Dad's shortcuts," they would often moan once awake.

Not this time. Tommy and I had abandoned the interstate shortly after entering the Florida Panhandle, opting to meander through the cotton fields, crops, and woods of rural Alabama and Mississippi on our way to Oregon. We stopped for gas, food, or water in tiny rural towns that seemed stuck in a time warp, seemingly unchanged for decades.

Our Independence Day together in the western North Carolina mountains two months earlier had been perfect—until now. Throat parched, ankles and back screaming, bug bites driving me mad, I leaned my back against a tree growing vertically out of the 45-degree-pitched slope we were climbing to take some of the weight off my legs if just for a few moments. Sweat poured down my face and out of every pore as I realized I was hyperventilating.

"It's got to be up here," Tommy shouted as he neared the top of the forested incline.

"Make sure," I yelled back. I was spent and miserable. How could I have been so stupid as to let him drag me so far up and so far off trail without enough water and the proper footgear?

We had begun the day in Asheville before venturing south into the Blue Ridge wilderness. We got a late start and the summer day was hot, so we decided to find a good spot to go river tubing instead of hiking. The problem was that there was almost no water flowing through the first river we found due to a severe drought.

"I hear the Green River still has plenty of water," said one of the guides at the first rafting outfitter. With that, Tommy drove his lime-green Subaru Forester south into the mountains while I checked potential destinations and routes on my phone. Before long, we were floating down the river in tubes, contentedly enjoying the peace, beauty, and refreshing water. By the time our two-to-three-hour excursion was over and we climbed back into the rickety, old school bus for the ride back to the starting point, my back was aching, and I'd already exhausted much more energy than during a typical day. Tommy had waterfalls on his mind for the next adventure.

"Look, I'm old, I'm heavy, and I'm not sure how much energy I have left to hike to a waterfall," I warned. "I'm all for finding a cool waterfall to check out, but it's got to be a short and relatively easy hike to get in and out."

"That's fine," he said.

When we struck out and were unable to locate the first trailhead we sought, we found a much larger falls described in a trail app, this one deeper into the mountains. We drove several miles down a gravel road, using hiker comments online to find the unmarked trailhead. At that point, we lost cell service and proceeded on faith. Not expecting to do any serious trekking, I hadn't even brought my hiking boots along. Instead I wore OluKais—good rubber tread underneath but a clog-like sandal on top with no ankle support. They were certainly not shoes suitable for climbing up and down steep grades through dense woodlands. About halfway to the waterfall, we ran into another couple on their way out.

"This way to the waterfall?" Tommy asked.

"Yes, it's straight up the trail," the woman answered.

"Is it worth it?" he asked.

"It's awesome," the man said. Eyeballing my size and footwear, he added, "But it's not easy. There's a rope to get down at one point."

As we proceeded up the trail, we began to hear running water. Relieved, I thought it was a short hike indeed. Unfortunately, particularly for the old guy of the duo, it was a river crossing we'd have to navigate before continuing. The depth, at about two feet, wasn't the issue; sloshing the rest of the way in soggy sandals was my biggest worry. Yet I also knew that trying to cross the slippery, hard rocks under the fast-moving water was not going to be easy. Even if my feet could take it, there was still the possibility of slipping and breaking an arm or cracking my head open. Slowly I was able to get myself across. But when we reached the falls the rope down was much more than I'd bargained for. Rather than the side-handrail-type rope I'd seen on the Appalachian Trail and elsewhere, this rope hung about thirty feet straight down a rock face, requiring you to rappel down.

"End of the line for me," I said.

"Are you sure?"

"I'm sure."

Tommy rappelled down much more quickly than I'd thought possible and soon disappeared into the woods. I found a rock to catch my breath and hydrate. Through the trees I could barely see the falls, which were beautiful, and I took pictures of wildflowers and the river. Then the black flies decided it was time to feast, and I was their main course. After what seemed like an eternity, Tommy scrambled back up the rock face, and we were on our way. We made a dumb mistake though by believing the trail made a huge loop and at some point meandered far from the trail that had led us there. For the next hour or more, we bushwacked our way up and down steep hill after steep hill, hanging on to trees to keep from tumbling down on several occasions.

Gasping for breath, the sun setting over the mountain, and with no way to summon assistance, I began to suspect we might be spending the night here.

"I'm sorry, Dad," Tommy said. "It's gotta be over this ridge."

"It's not your fault, it's both our faults. Let's just keep trying before we lose the sun altogether and have no direction to follow."

Just as darkness was falling, Tommy found the trail and led us out. By now I was limping, unable to speak beyond an occasional grunt, and hoping I had the strength to get back to the car. We had turned the "easy" 2.5-mile-round-trip hike following a very busy day into a 7-mile challenge course complete with ropes, river crossings, and hazards. The water back at the car never tasted better, and after watching the 4th of July fireworks finale from our car on the drive back into Asheville, the same could be said about the local craft brews.

We are all born with the need to be loved and affirmed, something I was becoming more and more attuned to while making up for lost time with Tommy. Whether you're a dockworker or a corporate chieftain, being recognized and accepted remains an important part of feeling you have value. When a father or mother spends quality time with a child, the activity doesn't matter nearly as much as the conversation and even silent time spent together. Receiving pats on the back, hugs, and other signs of approval from a parent are absolutely vital for a child to build confidence and self-worth. Without these, life is a much more difficult journey.

It was clear that July that the open communication and new relationship we'd developed in Orlando were paying off as we traveled toward Tommy's next chapter north of

Asheville. He was excited, cheerful, grateful, and thought-
ful. His silliness and constant attempts at making me laugh
were back, and although they at times bordered on being
annoying, this was far better and something I warmly accepted. It felt like we were making up for all the years we had
lost, and we found ourselves laughing, joking around, and
simply enjoying each other and the beauty of each day. This
camaraderie continued on our back-roads drive across the
continental United States a few months later. Tommy was
in a new place, and so was I.

The spiritual connection with nature that Tommy had
discovered at the beach continued to grow in North Carolina.
After detoxing at home with his beloved dog, Mo, and re-
claiming his belongings from pawnshops with Mike and me,
Tommy joined us on the drive to the annual music festival in
northern Florida. By now Mary was fully on board that what
he needed most was his family, and his father particularly,
she kept saying, and the four days together were relaxing
and fun. I spent one-on-one time with Tommy during several
sets of music throughout the festival. Although he was still
very fragile and a little paranoid that a laugh or comment
might be at his expense when it wasn't, he mostly seemed
relaxed and happy. He and our other sons and a couple of
their friends slept in tree hammocks or tents outside the adjacent RV spots we had secured. Mary would joyfully prepare
breakfasts and lunches for the masses each day, and the vibe
was positive throughout.

Tommy decided he wanted to take his love of nature to
another level by pursuing a career in organic farming. His
first job was on the edge of the Pisgah National Forest, a

mountainous area just east of Burnsville, North Carolina. He spent the remainder of the summer living and working on an organic farm in exchange for room and board. The agricultural science professor who owned and ran the place taught his green troupe such things as the difference between poisonous and nonpoisonous plants and which types of forest mushrooms and other legumes could be consumed, and exchanged a practical organic farming education for labor. About 85 percent of what the men and women working on the farm consumed each week was grown and prepared on the property, with the other 15 percent purchased in town weekly.

Similar farms existed elsewhere in the area, and on certain nights the entire community of mostly young men and women seeking a more natural and sustainable way of living came together to play music, sing songs, play volleyball, or just swap stories around a fire. Tommy loved it and fit right in. He told me it was the first time in his life he was surrounded by people who thought like him and the first time in his life he didn't feel judged by his wild hair, tattoos, or colorful clothing.

At the end of summer after the harvest, the professor, who was ready to return to college for the fall semester, asked Tommy if he wanted to stay on as caretaker for the winter. He briefly considered the offer. As the first autumn winds stirred the mountain air, members of Tommy's summer community scattered like the leaves floating from the trees. He wisely decided that he'd had enough isolation over the past few years and worried that spending the winter alone on a remote mountaintop was too risky and might trigger depression. After a brief conversation about this, I urged him to return home to see his dog, enjoy some of his mom's cooking, and spend time together. He agreed.

I told him how proud I was of him as I reflected how far he had come since his nearly fatal fall that spring. Both Mary and I were relieved and excited that he was coming home. It was time for Tommy to catch his breath.

24

TWENTY-FOUR
AND SO MUCH MORE

Tommy stood on the edge of the canyon, arms outstretched, briefly reminding me of a moment in the Who rock drama *Tommy* when Roger Daltry stood in a white, flowing, fringed shirt, arms similarly outstretched, his pinball disciples below.

Although Tommy had chosen the Rock and Roll Hall of Fame for a father-son outing years earlier when his namesake rock opera was the featured display at the time, today had nothing to do with then. Tommy was taking in huge gulps of the high desert air in the northwest corner of Colorado near the border of Utah. He was stunned by his first ever glance at the vast canyons and mesas created by the Colorado River over many centuries. He was connected with his spiritual center and drinking in every second of it.

Just a day earlier we had enjoyed a spectacular and challenging hike to both a waterfall and gorgeous lake nestled high in the Rockies of Rocky Mountain National Park. As in North Carolina earlier in the year, we had gone too far, pushed too hard, and run out of water. It was also far colder than anticipated, and as we emerged from the woods at sunset we both were chilled. At least this time I was wearing my hiking boots.

It struck me during the voyage westward that I was no longer teaching Tommy; he was now teaching me. Although he still had much to learn about the wilderness, beginning with always having enough water and wearing layers of clothing, particularly in high altitudes, his view of the world was beginning to make a lot of sense.

"You know, Dad, it's only been in this century that humans really started consuming more than they needed," he said during one of our long drives.

"That's not really true," I challenged him. "Look at the Vikings, the kings and queens of ancient times, the conquerors. All of them raided and killed for more land, more gold, more treasures, and more power."

"But that's not what I'm talking about."

"What are you talking about?"

"I'm talking about what has taken place in this country," he said. "Think about the Native Americans who used to live where we're driving right now. They only hunted what they needed and then ate or used every part of the animals they killed. Even in the times of the settlers, while there were bad guys, most people would use what they needed and share what they didn't with others in need."

"I kind of see what you mean," I said. "When I grew up in the country, people dropped everything to help a neighbor or stranger in need. It's why we had volunteer fire departments.

The horn would sound, and farmers would leave tractors in the field to rush to the firehouse and suit up."

"Exactly," he replied. "Today most people are only out for themselves and don't give a damn about anyone else. They will drive right by a car accident or old lady with a flat tire. They will steal from even their closest friends if they can get away with it. They eat and overeat from factory farms killing the planet, yet there are people going hungry. It's become messed up. That's what I'm saying."

"Well, how can you fix it?" I asked.

"One plastic bottle at a time," he smiled.

From the time we'd left Florida, the pile of plastic bottles on the floor behind his seat had been growing. In the over-packed Subaru, we barely had room for our belongings, yet the bottle mountain kept pushing higher. Tommy was incapable of walking by a discarded bottle or piece of litter on the ground without picking it up, something I admired about him. It was a huge shift from watching the adults of my youth tossing empty soda cans or beer bottles out the windows of their cars without a second thought. The famous ad with the tear rolling down the Native American's face came to mind. Tommy had determined that Mt. Plastic would continue to grow until we found a proper recycling can, which is still tough to find in economically depressed rural areas of the nation.

This was hardly the first time he'd pushed my thinking on environmental issues. "Time to get on the green path, Mom and Dad," was a popular refrain during his brief periods living at home.

By now Tommy had also become primarily vegetarian, except for occasionally eating chicken, which was not surprising given the circles of friends he'd made and the organic and natural life he aspired to. I knew it was only a matter of time before we'd be debating what he sees as ethical issues surrounding animal consumption.

"Hey, Dad, did you know that chickens are all shot up with hormones and unnatural chemicals so that the corporate chicken companies can make more profits?" he asked at another point. "And that they raise them in tiny cages so that they can't exercise, which might lower profits?"

"Yes, son, I've seen how chickens, cows, and other animals are harvested," I said, trying not to be goaded into a debate.

"Well, aren't you worried you are eating a bunch of chemicals and who knows what else?" he asked.

"I know you're right, but a lot of it comes down to price and how expensive organic proteins and veggies are," I said. "Even your generation throws all this concern out the window when it comes to getting a better price."

"Not me," he said, smiling, as if he could see he was starting to get under my skin.

"But you eat chicken; that must mean you're a hypocrite."

"Only chicken that is hormone free and naturally raised," he responded. "We had a neighboring farm in North Carolina where the chickens were raised the natural way, and taken one at a time only when needed for food. I saw how they were raised and harvested."

"Congratulations," I said.

"What?"

"You finally got to see where the term 'running around like a chicken with his head cut off' came from!"

We both laughed.

Conventional wisdom about the concepts of risk and education were other subjects we tackled during our trip to Oregon.

"Why is Mom so afraid of me camping or traveling alone?" he asked one day.

"Hello! Did you or did you not read *Into the Wild?*" I asked. "She is afraid you might die out there, that you might get hurt and not be found."

Both my wife and I had read the haunting bestseller about the affluent college kid who sold all his belongings, changed his name, and drifted for more than two years throughout the United States before hitchhiking to Alaska, walking into the wilderness, then dying alone. As our conversation continued, I recalled that Tommy now was exactly the same age as the subject of the book—twenty-four. He was also the same age as Neil Young in his presumably autobiographical song, "Old Man." As the song goes, "Old man, look at my life, I'm a lot like you were. . . . Twenty-four and there's so much more."[1]

Little did I know at the time, but Tommy's drifting phase was about to begin.

We pondered how a person is conditioned to avoid taking risks. It seems to be rooted in many of our earliest experiences. Kids fortunate enough to be loved and nurtured as youngsters are quickly taught to avoid taking risks because something bad might happen. The pressure from a persistent chorus of "don'ts" slowly wears down the carefree nature of most young children, replacing natural curiosity and daring with a fear of taking chances. "Don't climb so high on the monkey bars. Don't go outside without an adult. Don't get too close to that dog. Don't run." There's a fine line between protecting and smothering a child, I thought. The line between parental acceptance and indifference may be even thinner.

Suddenly, I saw two pairs of eyes in the pitch-black road ahead coming directly at us, jolting me from my silent musings. "Animals in the road," I shouted. Tommy immediately hit the brakes. The eyes, which seemed as high as the top of the Subaru's windshield, were actually higher than its roof. We were high up in the Colorado mountains, winding our way toward the exit of the national park from its remote southwestern corner, and had not seen another car in thirty minutes. Two massive bull elks were walking in our lane directly toward the front grill as if they were seeking a head-on collision. We'd been warned earlier in our travels that blowing the horn sometimes ticks an elk off. There have been cases where the animals have lowered their horns and done extensive damage to the offending car, particularly during mating season. Since Tommy's horn didn't work, this wasn't an option. Instead, we got an incredibly clear view of the impressive animals as they stepped nonchalantly into the beams of the headlights, looking down at the car, tiny by comparison, and then moved to the opposite lane and walked by.

"Incredible," Tommy said.

"Indeed," I said. "Glad we saw them because they were not going to move, and we wouldn't have stood a chance in a collision with those two."

We later returned to the topic of education, and I found myself agreeing with Tommy's logic.

"Why would I want to study organic farming or ag science in a classroom or trapped behind a computer when I have the opportunity to learn it firsthand?" Tommy asked. "On the farm, Mark showed us how to till, plant, cultivate, and harvest. We learned about growing seasons and the science of good crops versus bad crops. We learned how to make tea and various foods from plants growing wild in the forest. Being stuck in a kitchen or an office all day is not for me."

"I hear ya, son," I said. "But wouldn't it accelerate your desire to have your own organic farm some day by getting an associate's in ag science or something like that?"

"I don't really think so," he said. "Many of the people I'm learning from never finished college but have become successful farmers, brewmasters, and craftsmen. It's a new time, and there are tons of people out there like me that want to use only what we need and share the rest with others. I'm not interested in city living. I want to be close to and connecting with nature. I've never felt better than during the past few months."

"I get it, Tommy, and I'm proud of you."

"Thanks, Pops." He couldn't resist adding one more comment. "Remember, it's time to get on the green path before it's too late!"

Beyond the side trips to hiking trails, hot springs, waterfalls, and the occasional pilgrimage, such as the early morning visit to B.B. King's gravesite, the journey gave Tommy and me extensive time to connect more intensely and genuinely than ever before possible. We certainly didn't agree on everything, but we definitely gained deeper insights into each other's souls and beliefs. As each day passed, I realized that Mary had been right. He and I were the most alike in our family.

We had left Florida less than twenty-four hours after word came from a friend of Paul's that he had a good-paying job for Tommy on an organic vineyard outside of Portland. "But you need to get out here quickly," he told Tommy.

Early the next morning we pulled out of our driveway and were on our way to Oregon. I knew that it was my purpose to join Tommy on this journey, just as I know that God's purpose for me was to write this book, because it was the only week during the previous or following months that my schedule was essentially open. The "meant to be" doctrine that Mary had long believed in and that I had dismissed for years is certainly true. I now know this and only wish I'd opened my stubborn heart and mind sooner to accept it.

25

THE FLOW

As I sat in my chair at the beach, looking out over the water where Tommy was surfing, I reflected on the terrible journey he'd been through. Our family had been on a roller-coaster ride for nearly eight years now. Yet here I was, on a natural section of the seashore inside a national park, where there are no condominiums to cast shadows during the late afternoon sun. I rarely had been here, but Tommy insisted on it. It turned out to be well worth the five-dollar park fee and extra ten miles of driving.

Just like the little boy rolling in the sand many years earlier, Tommy seemed completely at peace when near the ocean. *Perhaps this is the higher power that had always seemed to elude him*, I thought, *his connection with the ocean*. The salty smell of the mist, the sound of waves breaking and seabirds calling, and the warmth of the sun made the beach a place like no other.

"Surfing is my high now," he said after emerging from the water, board under an arm displaying colorful images of his own design. "If I go surfing in the morning, I feel in a great mood all day and don't feel any need to get high. It's a natural high."

I later found out that it wasn't just the ocean that brought Tommy spiritual peace; all types of natural spaces lifted his soul, such as the cypress groves and state parks throughout central and northern Florida that most tourists never discover. He has been changed through experiences within the lush forests of North Carolina, Arkansas, and many other states. After we crossed the great Mississippi River, his eyes grew wide with wonder when he first set them on the Rocky Mountains. From waterfalls to mountain lakes to the spectacular desert vistas of Utah to the rain forests along the Washington/Oregon border where he worked in the vineyard, Tommy's psyche seems to have been rejuvenated. During our frequent phone calls, he's never seemed happier.

It is not as if he hasn't had bad days. On one such day I worried that the wheels might be coming off yet again—the worry coming from experience. But we find ourselves trying to break the habit of asking questions to gauge whether he is on the brink of another emotional breakdown that might lead to relapse. Such probes only serve to remind him of past failures or add more pressure about what might lie ahead. They do absolutely nothing to encourage where he is today and where many people wish they had the courage to be—living in the present.

When the organic vineyard in Oregon completed its seasonal harvest, Tommy decided it was time to move on. Mary and I were both distressed initially that again he had stayed in one place for only a short period. But after a poor first reaction, I righted myself quickly.

"Hey, just wanted to say I'm sorry about all the questions I was asking you yesterday. It had been a long day, and you caught me at a time when I was already tired and frustrated. I get it now."

"It's okay," he replied, the relief in his voice evident. "I just need a change."

He had been working long hours in a local coffee shop in addition to the outdoor job at the vineyard. As with previous restaurant jobs, I sensed he just wasn't cut out to work indoors for many hours at a time. Both employers said they'd welcome him back, he said, apparently at least having learned how not to burn his bridges by disappearing without notice.

"I'm starting to pick up some bad vibes in this area, and I'm not sure it's the right place for me," he continued.

"Help me understand."

"I don't know. I was talking for hours with my friend in California, and she told me I need to trust my senses. If I'm putting good vibes out there and not getting good feelings in return, I'm probably right and should try somewhere else."

This wasn't the first time we had discussed his hypersensitivity to other people and particular places. I now truly understood what he was saying. Since revitalizing our relationship, Tommy has taught me a lot about recognizing the positive and negative energy fields surrounding various people, places, and activities. When I thought hard about what he was saying, I recalled that I'd come across several books over the years basically saying the same thing and had even heard speakers talk about this. But unlike the rah-rah speech from a motivational speaker seeking to sell videos, books, or a program, Tommy's take was much more practical and sincere.

"It's all about surrounding yourself with positive people and environments," he explained, "and getting away from negative ones as quickly as possible."

"There are times, though, when it might just be in our heads," I said. "And there are other times when it is important to overcome negative people or experiences by either ignoring them or putting so much positivity out there that it turns things the other way."

"I understand and agree," he said. "What I'm saying is that I have to trust my instincts, and I'm picking up a lot of negativity around me lately. I feel I need to try somewhere else. It's all about the flow, Pops. I have to recognize the flow and go with it."

When I received the call, it made me worry he was near the brink again; he had sounded despondent. We talked at length, and by the end of the call he sounded much better. He was planning to camp for the night in the Mt. Hood area and had informed his bosses at both jobs that he needed a day off. By the following day, he was a different person; he was cheerful and mentally back on track. It was remarkable how much better twenty-four hours of connecting with nature had made him feel.

Though still disappointed he was leaving Oregon so quickly, a place where he had the support of two solid friends, one of whom we had known well for years, I understood. Working only indoors was crushing his spirit. The beginning of the gray, rainy Oregon winter certainly didn't help matters. He set out to explore areas he'd never before visited, traveling north to see volcanoes, more rain forests, and spectacular Pacific Ocean peninsulas. He also donated a bunch of clothes he rarely wore to a local Goodwill before leaving.

As I fielded his calls along the way, he raved about the spectacular hikes he was enjoying and adventures he was having. Now sleeping in his car when not in a state park or public campground, he was living his own version of Jack Kerouac's great *On the Road*, just as I had done over thirty years earlier. When I had hit the road after a college writing teacher encouraged this fantasy, I was twenty. Despite jeopardizing my ability to continue paying for my education at a private university, I felt that it was something I had to do. Whether this feeling was due to the adventurous, seemingly invincible nature typical of young men or to the need to overcome my childhood challenges, I didn't know. I just knew it was something no one could talk me out of. My late friend Dave, prone to crazy stunts that made my intended voyage look tame by comparison, was all in. I hitchhiked alone to Hartford, Connecticut, to get him, and after a night there the two of us set out with our sights on California. With both of us bearded, rough looking, and wearing black leather jackets, it's a wonder that anyone ever gave us a ride. But we made it to California and Mexico and eventually returned by way of the southern route across the country, experiencing many adventures along the way.

As Tommy's calls began coming in—from Washington, the beaches of Oregon, Lake Tahoe, Yosemite, Death Valley, Joshua Tree, and the beaches near San Diego—I realized he was on the same type of journey I'd taken so long ago. So what if he was four years older than I was? He had lost years to his drug abuse, and he was now seeking to reclaim them. California was as alluring to him now as it was to me then. Through my business travels we were able to connect in San Francisco, Monterey, and Las Vegas, leading to nearby hikes and adventures. He hiked the Grand Canyon, going to the bottom and back to the top in a day. He enjoyed the wonders of Bryce Canyon, Zion National Park, Arches National Park, and virtually any spectacular natural place he could find on his journey back east to North Carolina.

There are no such things as straight lines in the journey of life, and there certainly will be more hairpin curves and potholes in the years ahead. As each of us grows older, the best we can hope for is that our experience steering through prior accidents prevents us from running off the road too often. Nor is there any definitive handbook on parenting or managing family relationships, despite the shelves full of books on these subjects. As difficult as our middle son's challenges have been, the most remarkable and unexpected gift has come through a change in thinking that began with acceptance. The love was always there. Unconditional acceptance is something different and equally as powerful.

Obviously, our perspectives are our own, and each of us can hear only our own innermost thoughts. Our eyes see what we choose to see, and how we perceive things determines our choices along the way. These perceptions ultimately play a huge role in determining how happy and fulfilled we feel. However, when it comes to the most important relationships in our lives, those with our significant others and our children, it's not about us. The only thing we really have control over is how we choose to act or respond, whether we accept or reject their differences, and whether our words are kind or critical. Are we daily building them up or tearing them down, piece by piece, moment by moment? Are we willing to forgive mistakes and accept them no matter what? Are we committed to being present, not just physically but truly listening and with genuine love? When they have problems of inconceivable magnitude, do we wave the white flag or are we ready to get down in the trenches and fight for them?

From the time of his initial vanishing act related to hard drug use, California was never far from Tommy's mind. His favorite band was the Red Hot Chili Peppers. His favorite video games were tied to West Coast surfers, skateboarders, or snowboarders. Tommy had finally made it to the place he'd always dreamed of living.

Everywhere he went he managed to find the most beautiful and natural spots to lift his spirits higher. He excitedly shared each new epiphany and adventure. I had urged him to keep a journal so he could remember this incredible time in his life, and he started doing so. He added that he also was writing long letters that he planned to send to his mother and me. I told him not to worry too much about that and to focus on continuing to nurture his spiritual awakening.

As he rounded the highway curve and again laid eyes on the western rise of the Smoky Mountains, Tommy was so moved his eyes had filled with tears of happiness. And peace.

"I went to so many beautiful places and saw so many incredible things out west," he told us later. "But as soon as I saw the Smokies, I was overwhelmed with emotion. I just knew in my heart that this is where I'm supposed to be."

"You've taught me so much in the past few months," I said. "I'm so proud of how far you've come. Keep on growing."

"I just wanted to thank you for all you and Mom have done for me. I love you, Pops."

"I love you too, Tommy."

For the first time in years, I allowed hope to enter my spirit.

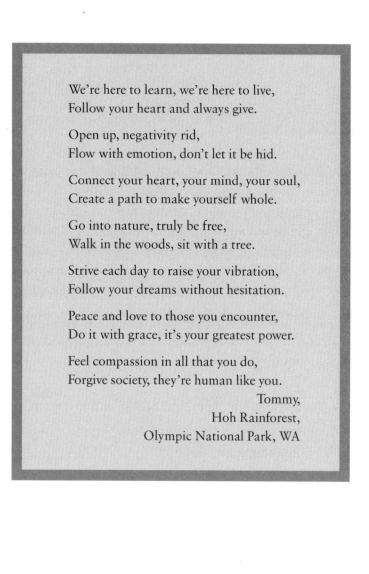

We're here to learn, we're here to live,
Follow your heart and always give.

Open up, negativity rid,
Flow with emotion, don't let it be hid.

Connect your heart, your mind, your soul,
Create a path to make yourself whole.

Go into nature, truly be free,
Walk in the woods, sit with a tree.

Strive each day to raise your vibration,
Follow your dreams without hesitation.

Peace and love to those you encounter,
Do it with grace, it's your greatest power.

Feel compassion in all that you do,
Forgive society, they're human like you.

Tommy,
Hoh Rainforest,
Olympic National Park, WA

NOTES

Chapter 1 The Vanishing

1. Mike Mariani, "How the American Opiate Epidemic Was Started by One Pharmaceutical Company," *Pacific Standard/The Week*, March 4, 2015, http://the week.com/articles/541564/how-american-opiate-epidemic-started-by-pharma ceutical-company.

2. Sheryl Gay Stolberg and Jeff Gerth, "High-Tech Stealth Being Used to Sway Doctor Prescriptions," *New York Times*, November 16, 2000, http://www .nytimes.com/2000/11/16/us/high-tech-stealth-being-used-to-sway-doctor-pre scriptions.html.

3. *Prescription Drugs: OxyContin Abuse and Diversion and Efforts to Address the Problem*, US General Accounting Office, Washington, DC, Publication GAO-04-110, December 2003, www.gao.gov/htext/d04110.html.

4. Chase Peterson-Withorn, "Fortune of Family behind OxyContin Drops amid Declining Prescriptions," June 29, 2016, Forbes, https://www.forbes.com /sites/chasewithorn/2016/06/29/fortune-of-family-behind-oxycontin-drops-amid -declining-prescriptions/#1e22a6a56341.

5. Elaine Silvestrini, "Florida Heals from Pill Mill Epidemic," Tampa Bay Times, updated August 31, 2014, http://www.tbo.com/news/crime/florida-heals -from-pill-mill-epidemic-20140830/.

6. *Results from the 2013 National Survey on Drug Use and Health: Summary of National Findings*, NSDUH Series H-48, HHS Publication No. (SMA) 14-4863, Rockville, MD: Substance Abuse and Mental Health Services Administration, 2014.

7. Pradip K. Muhuri, Joseph C. Gfroerer, and M. Christine Davies, *Associations of Nonmedical Pain Reliever Use and Initiation of Heroin Use in the United States,* Substance Abuse and Mental Health Services Administration, August

2013, http://archive.samhsa.gov/data/2k13/DataReview/DR006/nonmedical-pain
-reliever-use-2013.pdf.; Christopher M. Jones, "Heroin Use and Heroin Use Risk
Behaviors among Nonmedical Users of Prescription Opioid Pain Relievers—United
States, 2002–2004 and 2008–2010," *Drug and Alcohol Dependence* 132, nos. 1–2
(September 1, 2013): 95–100, doi.org/10.1016/j.drugalcdep.2013.01.007.

8. Results are from the 2014 National Survey on Drug Use and Health (NSDUH)
by the US Department of Health and Human Services. See *Prescription Drug Misuse and Abuse*, Substance Abuse and Mental Health Services Administration, updated October 10, 2015, https://www.samhsa.gov/prescription-drug-misuse-abuse.

9. Cassie Goldberg, "National Study: Teen Misuse and Abuse of Prescription Drugs Up 33 Percent Since 2008, Stimulants Contributing to Sustained
RX Epidemic," Partnership for Drug-Free Kids, April 22, 2013, https://drug
free.org/newsroom/news-item/national-study-teen-misuse-and-abuse-of-pre
scription-drugs-up-33-percent-since-2008-stimulants-contributing-to-sustained
-rx-epidemic/.

10. *From Rx to Heroin*, Partnership for Drug-Free Kids, the Medicine Abuse
Project, http://medicineabuseproject.org/assets/documents/Rx-to-Heroin.pdf.

Chapter 2 Despair aboard the Oxy Express

1. "Some Facts You Should Know about the History of Oxycodone," *A Forever
Recovery* (blog), September 21, 2014, http://aforeverrecovery.com/blog/informa
tion/facts-know-history-oxycodone/.

2. Barry Meier, "OxyContin maker to pay $600 million in fines," *New York
Times*, May 10, 2007, http://www.nytimes.com/2007/05/10/business/worldbusiness
/10iht-oxy.4.5655262.html.

3. Alex Morrell, "The OxyContin Clan: The $14 Billion Newcomer to Forbes
2015 List of Richest U.S. Families," Forbes, July 1, 2015, https://www.forbes.com
/sites/alexmorrell/2015/07/01/the-oxycontin-clan-the-14-billion-newcomer-to
-forbes-2015-list-of-richest-u-s-families/#151926675e02.

Chapter 6 Out of Sight, Out of Mind

1. *The Business of Recovery*, directed by Adam Finberg, http://www.thebusi
nessofrecovery.com/assets/bor_epress_kit_final.pdf.

2. Dan Munro, "Inside the $35 Billion Addiction Treatment Industry," Forbes,
April 27, 2015, https://www.forbes.com/sites/danmunro/2015/04/27/inside-the-35
-billion-addiction-treatment-industry/#55c457eb17dc.

3. National Institute on Drug Abuse, *Principles of Drug Addiction Treatment: A Research-Based Guide*, 3rd ed., https://www.drugabuse.gov/publications
/principles-drug-addiction-treatment-research-based-guide-third-edition/drug
-addiction-treatment-in-united-states.

4. Lance Dodes and Zachary Dodes, *The Sober Truth: Debunking the Bad
Science Behind 12-Step Programs and the Rehab Industry* (Boston: Beacon,
2014); "With Sobering Science, Doctor Debunks 12-Step Recovery," *All Things*

Considered, NPR, March 23, 2014, http://www.npr.org/2014/03/23/291405829/with
-sobering-science-doctor-debunks-12-step-recovery.

5. Treatment Statistics, National Institute on Drug Abuse, revised March 2011,
https://www.drugabuse.gov/publications/drugfacts/treatment-statistics.

Chapter 8 Boomerang of Agony

1. Opioid Overdose, Centers for Disease Control and Prevention, updated
September 26, 2017, https://www.cdc.gov/drugoverdose/epidemic/index.html.

Chapter 10 Rise of the Opioid Kids

1. Liz E. Whyte, Geoff Mulvihill, and Ben Wieder, "Politic of Pain: Drugmak-
ers Fought State Opioid Limits amid Crisis," Center for Public Integrity, updated
December 15, 2016, https://www.publicintegrity.org/2016/09/18/20200/politics
-pain-drugmakers-fought-state-opioid-limits-amid-crisis.

2. Harriet Ryan and Kim Christensen, "Amid Opioid Epidemic, Rules for
Drug Companies Are Loosened," *Los Angeles Times*, July 27, 1016, http://www
.latimes.com/local/california/la-me-pharma-bill-20160728-snap-story.html.

3. "Florida Drug Database and 'Pill Mill' Regs Curbed State's Top Opioid Prescribers, Study Suggests," Johns Hopkins University Bloomberg School of Public
Health, June 2, 2016, http://www.jhsph.edu/news/news-releases/2016/florida-drug
-database-and-pill-mill-regs-curbed-states-top-opioid-prescribers-study-suggests
.html; Hsien-Yen Chang et al., "Impact of Prescription Drug Monitoring Programs
and Pill Mill Laws on High-Risk Opioid Prescribers: A Comparative Interrupted
Time Series Analysis," *Drug and Alcohol Dependence* 165 (August 1, 2016): 1–8,
doi.org/10.1016/j.drugalcdep.2016.04.033.

Chapter 16 Beyond Twelve Steps: The Business of Recovery

1. Jonathan Rothwell, "Drug Offenders in American Prisons: The Critical Dis-
tinction between Stock and Flow," Brookings Institution, November 25, 2015, https://
www.brookings.edu/blog/social-mobility-memos/2015/11/25/drug-offenders
-in-american-prisons-the-critical-distinction-between-stock-and-flow.

Chapter 22 The Path to Acceptance

1. Rose A. Rudd et al., "Increases in Heroin Overdose Deaths—28 States, 2010
to 2012," Centers for Disease Control and Prevention, *Morbidity and Mortality
Weekly Report* 63, no. 39 (October 3, 2014): 849–54, http://www.cdc.gov/mmwr
/preview/mmwrhtml/mm6339a1.htm?s_cid=mm6339a1_w.

Chapter 24 Twenty-Four and So Much More

1. Neil Young, "Old Man," on *Harvest*, recorded February 6, 1971, Reprise
Records, Quadrafonic Sound Studio, Nashville, TN.

Rick Van Warner has more than three decades of experience as a journalist, crisis-management counselor, and media-relations expert, honing a critical eye into some of the most difficult challenges of our time. His book on the nation's growing opioid epidemic was spurred by his family's personal experience and his heartfelt calling to help other families wrestling with similar issues. *On Pills and Needles: The Relentless Fight to Save My Son from Opioid Addiction* details his son's harrowing eight-year fight to survive Oxycontin and later heroin abuse, while providing a compelling look behind the curtain of an epidemic created by pharmaceutical-industry greed and inept government oversight.

A graduate of Syracuse University's S.I. Newhouse School of Communications, Van Warner began his career as a daily newspaper reporter. Always willing to tackle tough challenges, he also volunteered as a social worker within the New York State youth justice division, where he counseled teens confined to group homes after committing serious crimes.

After working for many years as a journalist and editor in New York City, Van Warner shifted to an executive role in corporate communications and crisis management to create more time for his four children and coaching various youth sports. In addition to his writing endeavors, he remains active as a consultant and speaker.

Van Warner and his wife of thirty-two years currently reside in central Florida.